Voices in the

John Bowden

*Voices in
the Wilderness*

SCM PRESS LTD

334 01746 7

First published 1977 by
SCM Press Ltd
56 Bloomsbury Street London WC1
Second impression 1978

Filmset in 'Monophoto' Ehrhardt 10 on $11\frac{1}{2}$ pt by
Richard Clay (The Chaucer Press), Ltd, Bungay, Suffolk
and printed in Great Britain by
Fletcher & Son Ltd, Norwich

Stets Gewohntes nur magst du verstehn:
doch was noch nie sich traf,
danach trachtet mein Sinn.

Contents

	Preface	ix
1	Change or Decay?	1
2	Honest to God?	14
3	What Happened to the New Reformation?	28
4	Beyond Belief?	42
5	Come to Church	58
6	Voices in the Wilderness	72
	Notes	83

Preface

Virtually all those who have read the typescript of this book have told me that it is depressing. I have not found it at all easy to write, although I have done my best to make it straightforward to read. I hope that the text speaks for itself. But perhaps I should make one thing clear. The negative comments which you will find here do not arise as a projection of personal depression on to the state of the churches. I have simply tried to present what I see and think and believe.

Over the months while the book has been in the making I have been through a whole gamut of emotions. Some sections have been rewritten many times. What has survived has been considered and reconsidered in misery and in happiness, and to that degree may, I think, claim a degree of objectivity. The latter was uppermost as I went through the typescript for the last time, but there was still much gloom which I felt unable to remove. I am especially fortunate in knowing something of the loving and sharing and being reconciled in the truth which seems to me to lie at the heart of the gospel; it is impossible not to be saddened and angered by all that so hinders it elsewhere, and especially in the life of the church.

JSB

I

Change or Decay?

Go down the steep and narrow lane from Highgate village, turn right through the wrought iron gates and climb the hill again behind the high brick wall and you have left London behind. You are in another world and another age. Vegetation chokes the old memorials and the roots of trees tilt them to crazy angles; a generation of neglect has produced a woodland wilderness. Go on a damp, misty November day with the rain dripping down from the trees and the overpowering smell of deadness and decay, and you are back in the last century. So great is the change as you walk along the twisting path that anything might happen, so it is no surprise to turn a corner and find what looks like the entrance to an Egyptian temple. Within its precincts, suburban families have continued their attempt to preserve the illusion that death is only another form of this life, with their neat tombs built like little houses, complete with front door and keyhole, fronting both sides of a circular avenue. Outside, among the narrow walks, familiar names suddenly catch the eye: Victorian novelists like John Galsworthy and Mrs Henry Wood; Landseer the artist and Carl Rosa the impresario; Michael Faraday the pioneer in electricity and Sir Rowland Hill who began the penny post.

The old part of the cemetery is usually closed to the public now, which adds to the sense of desolation and loneliness for those who do manage to be allowed in. Over the road, in the newer part, the atmosphere is much less dank and forbidding. The graves are cared for and the scenery is less bizarre; among the monuments on the main drive there is one that towers above all the rest: a gigantic stone head of Karl Marx, set on a great pedestal, and beneath it some words from his famous 'eleventh thesis on Feuerbach':

The philosophers have only interpreted the world in various ways; the point, however, is to change it.

We go to see Karl Marx quite often. We live within walking distance, and many of our visitors want to look at his memorial. I have grown quite fond of the place; it is impossible not to be moved by the constantly changing tokens of remembrance at the foot of the pedestal, the messages and fresh flowers left from all over the world. And even for those who would not call themselves Marxists, it is impossible when there not to reflect on the changes for which Marx was indeed responsible, the influence which has stretched out from the British Museum reading room to the furthest corners of the modern world.

Looking round at the sea of stone crosses and up at the silhouettes of the churches on the horizon, it is impossible, too, not to have other thoughts, especially if you are a Christian constantly forced to ask yourself questions. Christianity also changed the world. In a way more impressive even than Karl Marx, the first followers of Jesus presented their remarkable message of a crucified saviour, whose life, lived out in utter commitment to his teachings, was the spark for a dynamic movement which captured an empire. Against all the odds it was carried to the ends of the known world because of its claim to know the true nature and purpose of the universe, and because it too was capable of embodying its teachings in a common way of life characterized by openness, compassion and care. The people of Thessalonica put it as well as anyone, when Paul's mission arrived at their doors: 'These men who have turned the world upside down have come here also.'

The power of Marxism is still strong, that of Christianity waning. Whatever the community may have been, in Britain as it approaches its two thousandth birthday it has seen better days, and those who take its temperature and feel its pulse are not encouraging. For the most part their prognosis is gloomy and

2

their tone sombre. The churches, these commentators have been arguing for years, cannot survive for very long in their present form. They are smitten with a chronic lingering disease. Perhaps the only way in which they can continue in existence is to concentrate all their vigour on their own survival, detaching themselves, as some chronic invalids tend to, from what is going on around them and instead being in the main preoccupied with their own state of health and their own confined existence.

Any case that might be put for the other side has gone by default. There are no longer confident voices boldly announcing that despite the appearances all is well with the churches, and giving convincing reasons for their views. Some may be more confident about a future for individual, personal religious belief, or for particular forms of Christianity which sit lightly to the organized churches, but that is about all. The churches are indeed dying and the statistics are there to confirm what first-hand impressions convey. Leave Karl Marx and walk up the road into the rarified heights of Highgate, or go down into the urban jungle of Islington, Tufnell Park and Camden Town; talk privately to the Rural Dean of West Haringey or the Bishop of Edmonton and press them for their frank opinions. They – and their opposite numbers in other churches – are hardly likely to give you messages of good cheer. And the situation is likely to be similar in most of the towns and cities in Great Britain. Of course there are isolated successes: parishes do flourish, Christianity comes alive. But these are the exceptions.

Dying churches are not abstractions. They bring with them real personal suffering and anguish. Statistics are not just figures; they represent real people, dashed hopes, failed expectations. And as one comes to terms with this particular pattern of death it is more comfortable not to have too vivid an imagination, too deep a sense of involvement or too good a view.

Highgate is a good place for seeing things from. Set on the highest land in North London, lived in by particularly friendly people who have acquired a reputation for being something of an intellectual elite, fringed with attractive woods and the wide expanse of Hampstead Heath, it is a privileged place. And it affords marvellous views over London. You can see only a few of the famous sights; from here, rather, the impression of London is that of a vast, impersonal, lonely place. Out there, if anywhere, is a crying need for what the Christian churches might offer, for the sense of fellowship, community and family of which the Christian gospel speaks. It does not take much to think of the cumulative loneliness there can be for those without families, with few friends and disinterested neighbours, and of the relatively scarce opportunities there are for a sense of belonging and involvement to develop. Here and there are the church towers and spires and domes, but instead of pointing to a centre of love and outgoing pastoral concern they are likely to announce the presence of little more than a scattering of long-term residents whose association with the church stops at sparsely attended weekly worship, and coffee mornings, jumble sales and bazaars. Their potentialities are somehow stuck at the level of their own narrow concerns, their own parochial problems; their expectation of an increase of numbers, let alone of changing anything, is minimal. How many thousands have these groups failed in their time, without perhaps even having realized the fact? How many have they never even begun to care for? How many have they never been remotely capable of attracting, or have they turned away simply because they could not even listen? And how much have they taken for granted? How many questions have they asked about themselves and the state that they are now in?

But it would be unfair to make the criticism too sharp. Perhaps such churches have never been helped to think, to see what they might be doing. When the structure of the church building remains the same and the pattern of the church's activities remains the same and what is said in the name of Christianity remains the same, year in and year out, it is possible to become isolated from what is going on in the world outside, cocooned within an insulated capsule. And the threat of death is one from stifling and suffocation, requiring quite remarkable leadership to show a way of breaking out.

The trouble is that no single cause is responsible for this depressing situation, which has grown up over generations, and those who might be expected to show a lead, the clergy, are if anything caught up in its snares even more than their congregations. After all, congregations can just stop going to church; for the clergy it is a livelihood, and though they may despair of exercising any kind of effective ministry and feel tempted to throw in the sponge, there is often nowhere they might go.

This side of clergy life is still far too little thought about. The characteristics of the stock Anglican parson as portrayed in comedy and caricature are familiar enough; so too is the more generous picture of the devoted pastor. Under the surface, however, the reality may be very different. Ministers are not set apart from their fellow men to that degree, as either less than seriously human or as superhuman figures. The dying churches include men like those who spoke to Leslie Paul, writing an official report on the deployment of the clergy in 1965, of breakdown, despair, fighting demons, suicide. Or the thirty per cent of those taking part in a more recent informal survey who indicated that they felt that no one in authority cared what happened to them. Perhaps such pictures of the clergy would be unfamiliar and even shocking to the congregations in their charge, who are all too likely to think of them as made in a different mould, freed from the more desperate human feelings. Perhaps they have not stopped to consider what may happen when a man has demands made on his early dedication and idealism which he is simply unable to bear, when he is thrust into a situation not of his own making, far from his expectations and over which he has no control.

Outspoken public testimonies about such men are rare. They take a lot of making. But once made they are difficult to forget. I cannot put out of my mind one picture drawn by an understanding clergy wife, though it is several years since I first read it. It is Saturday night and her husband is crying in her arms in despair because he has two sermons to preach the next day and nothing at all to say. His mind is blank – no thought, no words. The appointed lessons seem to say nothing to him, and worse than that, he is acutely aware of his own emptiness – as though he himself had no real being. The feeling comes to him often. At other times it can take the form of an utter lack of direction, as though he

5

were wandering alone in some unsignposted wilderness with no indication of what he should do, where he should go or what he should become.

And yet in spite of this the life of the parish has to go on. The sermons have to be preached, the church roof has to be propped up if it is falling down. People come to him for advice and expect him to know the answers; he has to try to mediate the love of God to them, however little he is aware of it himself. No wonder they are beginning to ask how good he is. He asks himself the same question and answers it as they do.[1]

Some priests do not have an understanding wife with whom to share their burden; some do not have the insight or the courage to realize just who they are and what they have become. Psychology has taught us a lot about the devious workings of human personality and the lengths to which we will go to disguise unpleasant truths from ourselves. So it is possible to recognize similar sufferers who perhaps may not even be aware of their ailment, except perhaps as some kind of malaise. There are those who conceal their real problems by refusing to ask questions and viciously attacking those who do, who fill the emptiness with overwork, disguise the hollowness inside them by keeping to the public repetition of the same tired formulae, the same stereotyped phrases, or who concentrate simply on keeping the machinery going.

And yet it is the machinery which creates the problems. The antiquated parish pattern, impossible to work properly in urbanized Britain, the ties and the restrictions of old buildings in the wrong place – the details have been repeated ad nauseam. Or the stereotyped pattern of church activities, virtually all taken over from the past without very much reflection, from public worship to parish fete. Or the regional organization of administration into dioceses and synods. Or, above all, the quite appalling working conditions at the local level. What modern business would expect its employees to work in the way that the clergy are made to? What organization would continue such a system with so few questions about their purpose and their effectiveness, encouraging those personal idiosyncracies which make it so difficult for clergy to co-operate with each other, while ignoring their isolation, and thus in effect abdicating virtually all corporate responsibility? And what is the justification in any common-sense terms for the use of so many expensive resources in so haphazard a way with so little machinery for adapting to such a rapidly changing world.?

Again, what organization would tolerate for so long the tangible results of such a desolating situation? It has been obvious for a long time, as many bishops and theological principals could point out, that the most able members of the church are no longer offering themselves for ordination. They seem to feel that they can best use their gifts in other directions. Of those who do begin ordination training, or who choose to read theology at a university, once more it is often the best who then follow some other vocation. And the number of those who are in fact ordained and after a few years 'drop out', to take up some other work, is extraordinarily high.

The pattern even continues to the top. It would be unrealistic to say that, for example, the bishops of the Church of England as a group represent the best leadership the church could have; it is certain that there are distinguished men who could have done much in this direction but who have refused elevation to the episcopate, even when it has been offered to them through the present far from satisfactory system of appointment. Nor can those who knew and loved him ever forget the last years of the man whose acceptance of the see of Durham proved to be a sentence of death.

The churches do a great deal to create their own hells. And those in positions of authority do not seem to care. Of course, many of them do, inwardly and personally. But there is no effective, public, recognizable expression of that care. It seems indeed to be thought bad form to point out the problems, and they do not figure very largely in church newspapers, ecclesiastical debates or official pronouncements.

If the churches are so ineffective at even thinking of how to change themselves, and if their own situation is so grave, how can they be instruments for changing other people or the world?

Perhaps the churches should die. Perhaps they really are fighting

7

a losing battle, and nothing can save them as they are. Perhaps they were the product of a particular period and now have had their day. It may be, again as the commentators keep saying, that they are surviving only on past capital, material and intellectual, which in due course will run out. The sociologists and historians who forecast the patterns of the future may well be right.

The churches as they now are cannot survive for very long. Nor should we wish to prolong their life beyond the point at which new and more viable forms of Christian life have become apparent. Indeed what is to be feared is rather that the present churches, unadapted to the new age, *will* contrive to survive – but by going culturally underground and becoming totally irrelevant to the on-going life of mankind. In these days when the obsolescence of the church's modes of thought and life is so painfully evident, but while there is still no vision of the right ways in a changing world, it is increasingly difficult for Christians acutely aware of the need for new forms to continue within the old. There has accordingly been a dramatic drop in the number of candidates for the Christian priesthood and ministry and a continuous movement out of these vocations into forms of secular service. And the resulting danger is that as the more radical spirits leave it the church will thereby become more and more conservative and defensive so that instead of transforming itself it will persist as a spiritual ghetto, fundamentalist in thought and pietistically criticizing a world which it cannot understand.[2]

Suppose that this is not an unfair picture of the situation, and that the dramatic drop includes not only the clergy but the laity; when someone reaches the point of feeling that they can accept the pattern of church life no longer, where is he or she to go? Alternative groups of Christians are formed from time to time, but they are fragile, and are put under great pressure by the tendency of members to move elsewhere or by the demands made by work and other responsibilities. Or it is possible for an individual to work out a personal life-style and to attempt to find a deeper religious understanding by reading, thinking, meditating and praying, with perhaps an occasional visit to a church. But this is a lonely and discouraging type of faith. Christianity, after all, is essentially a way of life to be shared.

Furthermore, any attempt at an alternative pattern alongside the institutional churches at the same time throws their failings into relief. Alternative groups are usually small, poor, with very few material resources, perhaps even finding difficulty over somewhere to meet. While evident everywhere is all that organization, all that heritage, all those possessions, dominated by so cramping a framework, with comparatively speaking so little achievement to show. Cannot better use be made of that?

And in any case, when there is really nowhere else to go, opting out seems to be a final confession of defeat. Moreover, since many of us have grown up within churches and have been shaped by them, the thought of opting out brings with it a sense of loss, the prospect of abandoning part of ourselves that has very deep roots. Above all, opting out seems an admission that change really is an ideal dream, although change is cried out for. And so some of us remain, feeling frustrated and ineffective, scattered here and there, knowing that we are not quite alone in the way we feel about things, but deprived of any way of making our feelings known and attempting to discover if they are shared even more widely. We may feel that our voices are indeed little more than voices in the wilderness, vainly crying where no one will listen. And our sense of isolation may grow so strong that we begin to wonder whether, despite all the arguments to the contrary, we may not in the end be better outside the churches than in.

The churches primarily need to change because they are such inefficient means of showing the care and the concern and the possibilities for love and reconciliation and forgiveness which they profess. It was through all these things that they began to change the world and it is not least because of a failure in them that they are dying. But Christians began to care as they did because through Jesus they had a new vision of the world and what it might be, a new understanding of man's nature and destiny and purpose which they struggled to express in terms that could be understood by very different cultures. Their care was the medium

9

of a message. The gospel was reinterpreted as it spread from Palestine to Greece and Rome and further afield, and found expression not only in new languages but also in new ideas. It was, moreover, seen as a matter of vital concern. Christians really acted as though God and eternity, life and death were at stake.

Here too, things are not as they were, and senility has set in. Much of the same language is still used, but it no longer has quite the same ring about it. It is not only the case, as so often, that the promise and assurance expressed fit so badly with the reality. Often the language and the ideas are quite incomprehensible or irrelevant to the vast majority. In most Christian churches the pattern of belief, like the patterns of other activities, seems to be taken over automatically from the past, without a great deal of thought. The statements of Bible and creeds, the existence of an ordained ministry, the forms of worship, may be interpreted and regulated in different ways, but essentially their significance and their place is taken for granted. They are part of the total picture, like the rest of the fabric and the furniture.

Inherited belief has given the churches the shapes they now possess. Inherited belief determines church organization and church activities. Inherited belief determines people's attitudes and shapes their habits. Within the churches it serves as an unquestioned support for maintaining things as they are. For surely, the strongest argument for perpetuating the churches in something like their present form would seem to be that for all their faults they are preserving essentials of the Christian heritage which would otherwise be lost. And though this argument is seldom put explicitly, its validity is taken for granted, and life goes on and on as it is, under its old momentum.

Now if keeping the churches in their present form really is the best way of preserving the truth of the Christian gospel, and this could be explained convincingly, the current situation in the churches might be just about tolerable. But there is another disturbing indication. Not only are the churches failing to care about people, they are also failing to care sufficiently about the truth. And if that is in fact the case, they really have become what their critics have been claiming, no more than decadent institutions, selfishly fighting for their own survival.

There are some unpleasant symptoms. First, after a theological upheaval of unprecedented dimensions little over ten years ago, the churches now seem to be heading back to a new conservatism as though nothing had happened. Secondly, although there is the unquestioned assumption that all is still well with traditional belief, there is less actual talk about it and teaching of it than there ever was. The availability of books, the obvious teaching medium, makes this plain enough. It is possible to find scholarly books which give historical explanations for the development of various features of Christian life and thought, but there is little which explains in comprehensible terms how even the well-educated reader can begin to understand what they mean now.

For example, over the past ten years there have been unprecedented changes in the way in which the eucharist is celebrated, and there are little books which explain why these changes have been made. But what is the eucharist and what does it mean today? Here the literature is silent. Baptism is administered indiscriminately to large numbers in a way which proves to be little more than a formality. Because the highest theological significance is accorded to it in many quarters, parish clergy consequently have crises of conscience. But what is baptism? Again, ministers are clearly puzzled over the role that they should be playing in a society where so many of their former functions have been taken over by others: what is the nature of ordination, and precisely what is it that sets an ordained priest apart? The silence persists.

There are a great many questions of this sort which I find it extremely difficult to answer, despite my theological training. The terms which would make most sense to me would call for changes in church order and existing church regulations. There is a great deal that I find difficult to justify as things are. I have taken to cross-questioning friends in conversation and have found that many of them are just as uncertain as I am, whether they are ordinary members of congregations or the occupants of senior academic or ecclesiastical positions. And I have found this situation reflected in some of the books which have given me most help and encouragement over recent years. One could make a list of some of the new classics of Christian writing: Harry Williams, *The True Wilderness*; John Austin Baker, *The Foolishness of God*; John Taylor, *The Go-Between God*; Hans Küng, *On Being a Christian*. None of them have much to say, except in criticism, about the formal expressions of belief as made in church order. For all these books, as (one suspects) for those who read them, the focal point of concern lies somewhere else. The other aspects are by no means as important for us as they once were.

That is not to say that we are right. Nor is it to say that baptism, the eucharist, the ministry do not matter. But it does suggest that they need to be thought about a good deal harder. And it suggests that a new look is necessary at the setting in which they are placed, the way they are administered and the interpretation which is given to them. The old inherited explanations are no longer good enough. New ones are needed, and because they are concerned with practical matters, they are likely to imply change.

What is fatal at present is the superficiality with which the whole *raison d'être* of the church is treated, and the absence of any tangible attempt at deep thought. At best there is acceptance, apathy and disinterest, and at worst a kind of duplicity where certain thoughts are harboured in private but not allowed public expression for fear of the damage that might be done to the 'faithful'. Equally appalling is the failure to recognize the workings of a new spirit of love and growing together and sharing and deepening experience, if it does not happen to bear the usual conventional labels. Time and again, far more importance is attached to form than to content.

As will be clear by the end of this book, there is no suggestion here that all is up with Christianity or that God is no longer at work in the way Christians have believed him to be active in the past. But for too long the churches have been far too confident about prescribing the modes of divine activity, and now their over-confidence is beginning to catch up with them, threatening to leave them with a hollow shell. The containers into which new workings of the spirit might flow are quite inadequate. The tangible means of expressing new insights are too restricted. And this situation can be remedied only by much deeper thinking than is evident in the churches and a much greater desire for radical change.

For these reasons, this is essentially a book of questions. Asking questions can be a dangerous matter. Those who engage in it can be accused of sowing unnecessary doubt and dismay, indeed of destructiveness. I hope that these particular questions are not viewed in that light. They are asked with a purpose. It may be that answers can be given to some of them, either by changing the way things are done or by providing more satisfactory explanations. In which case, let that happen. It can only be for the better. Or there may be no answer to them at all. If that is the case, then let us live with our uncertainty, without pretending to a kind of knowledge that we do not, or cannot, have. In any event, things will begin to happen to us only when we recognize the truth of how we are and how things are. Nothing lasting can be based on an illusion.

It is impossible to care for people better by writing books. Caring is caring. Loving is loving. But if a rethinking of belief can help to reshape the way in which Christianity is expressed, then theory and theology may have their place. The issue is one that we shall have to take up in more detail, together with a number of dimensions of Christianity which may be thought to have been ignored, in the last chapter.

Meanwhile, there is a good deal that we have to look at rather more closely. So first we shall indulge in some of the nostalgia that has become so fashionable – not for some golden age but for the period a little over ten years ago, when it seemed as though the questions hinted at here would really be tackled and some changes would really be made. We shall look first at the intellectual crisis symbolized by *Honest to God* and then at the hopes for a new church expressed in the ideas of a 'new Reformation'. After that we shall look more closely at the nature of the Christian heritage, to see just what the Christian churches value so highly. How much would they really risk losing if they were willing to undergo a marked change? This will involve us in considering first the more abstract area of Christian doctrine and then the visible expressions of belief in the existence of the church itself, its ministry and sacraments.

13

2

Honest to God?

Its suddenness and the way in which it developed took everyone by surprise.

On 17 March 1963, in what now seems like another age, the Sunday newspaper *The Observer* gave pride of place to an article by John A. T. Robinson, then Bishop of Woolwich, under the title 'Our Image of God must Go'. The article, replacing at short notice another feature which had failed to materialize, gave unexpected publicity to a small paperback by Dr Robinson which appeared the following Tuesday, and in consequence helped to trigger off a religious debate unparalleled in the present century. It seems unlikely that the author would have attracted quite so much publicity had he not been a bishop in the Church of England and therefore officially responsible for upholding belief in God rather than appearing to demolish it; it is also unlikely that the book he wrote would have captured the public's imagination quite so much had it not been given the brilliant title *Honest to God*.

Honest to God made its impact first and foremost by the questions it asked about the way in which modern man might still find it possible to think about God. Is he out there, or in here? Can the language in which Christians have spoken of God in the past still make sense to modern man? Is it not necessary now to find some new imagery, a new vocabulary? In particular, Dr Robinson suggested that to talk of 'the ground of our being' might make better sense than any imagery which suggested that God was up in the sky.

Honest to God also asked questions about man. Is modern man still religious, does he still have a 'God-shaped blank' within him, or have we now seen the development of a new 'secular' man, who feels that he can get on perfectly well without religion, without a desire for personal salvation, without a sense of sin?

Against this background it raised some other important questions. If our image of God must go, and modern man is secular, what does that mean for our understanding of Jesus, the traditional practices of prayer and worship, the time-honoured ways of thinking about right and wrong?

The ideas expressed in *Honest to God* were not particularly new; most of them had been in the air for some time. But *Honest to God* focused in a special way the feelings of the time. The consequences of its publication were amazing. All at once it made everyone talk about the questions it raised. And they did so avidly, often apoplectically, at great length and throughout the world. As well as being a topic of conversation and discussion inside and outside the churches, the book was reviewed and featured in all the national papers, on radio and television. The debate soon spread to America, and *Honest to God* was rapidly translated into German, French, Swedish, Dutch, Danish, Italian and Japanese (yet more languages followed later). A story even went the rounds that news of it had reached the Kremlin via a Swedish newspaper.[1]

For many people within the churches *Honest to God* was inspired by the devil. This was evident from the hostile letters they wrote to newspapers, and there were reviews, like those in *The Times* and *The Sunday Telegraph*, which supported them in this view. Others, picking up a theological book for the first time in their life, found it heavy going; many of them clearly failed to understand it and abandoned it before the end. Those who did read theological books at all regularly were often at a loss to see what all the fuss was about. Since much of the contents of *Honest to God* had been familiar to teachers and students in universities and theological colleges for some time, the book did not seem at all shocking, or even radical. If anything, they found it difficult to assimilate because it appeared to be muddled and evasive in so many of its arguments, and even distasteful in the way in which it sought to bring together in one heady cocktail ingredients which, to their more sophisticated palates, simply should not have been mixed.

However, all this is relatively unimportant. It is notable how many of the published reviews, for all their hesitations and qualifications, in fact welcomed and endorsed the line of questioning which had been opened up. And the really important consequence was that a significant number of people clearly sensed what they felt to be a kindred spirit articulating questions which had nagged away at the back of their minds, half formed. They had their own contribution to make as well. So while there was savage attack on Dr Robinson and energetic defence, blast and counter-blast, in the background there was a continuous if somewhat incoherent conversation about the truth of Christian belief, often going away at a tangent, but still returning again and again to fundamental religious questions. And there was undeniable evidence that the world was not divided neatly into believers and unbelievers, members of the church and non-members, but that the lines were blurred. A significant number of people felt themselves to be neither in one camp nor the other, were not quite sure just where to go next, but were searching for a viable alternative to the institutional religion and the doctrinal theology that they were being offered.

Against this background, the details of what was actually said in *Honest to God* were of secondary importance. It served so to speak as a fuse to detonate a considerable explosion. The impressive thing was the way in which it triggered off a 'great debate' which then took on its own momentum. In addition to causing offence and arousing fear, it also brought liberation and a sense of relief to those who had long found the atmosphere of the churches stifling, and had been particularly alienated by doctrinal statements and intellectual assumptions which they were often unable to make sense of, let alone accept.

A search for truth was on, and it is heartening to recall the words of a man who might have been expected to sympathize more with the hostility of *The Times* and *The Sunday Telegraph* than with the views of the Bishop of Woolwich. Sir Alec Douglas Home, then Foreign Secretary in the Conservative government, told the General Assembly of the Church of Scotland: 'Too often the simple, basic teachings are overlaid by doctrine and dogma against which the intelligence revolts. Books like *Honest to God* show that there is a passionate desire that religion should appeal to the mind. Do not let us fear this search for the truth.'[2]

The search continued. The relatively slow process of book publication took up the broadcasts and the newspaper articles and carried them further, and the subject matter was spread wider. A small flood of paperbacks contributed to the 'ferment in the church' and the circulations of the journals in which 'radical' Christians had been exchanging their views began to boom. A brand new one, *New Christian*, appeared, and quickly became a focal point for the mood of the time.

Of course one should not over-romanticize what had begun to happen. Only a relatively small proportion of the population was involved. Public debate is never a very satisfactory way of carrying on serious discussions. And inevitably the debate had its silly side, as in the literature which mushroomed, especially in America, in connection with a 'death of God' theology. If *Honest to God*, as its author conceded, had never been the most readable of books, many discussions of it by professional theologians must have been impossible for the untrained reader to make head or tail of. But again, if one returns to the writing of the time, wades through the ephemera and the irrelevant arguments which were produced, there is no mistaking behind it all a sense of exhilaration, a mood of expectancy. At last something was going to happen, there was going to be a breakthrough, the moulds were cracking, a new age would shortly be dawning.

That seems to be the key to the episode. Here was no abstract, academic debate, but something which amounted to an intellectual crusade. It looked as if a third force between the traditionalists and the uninterested might be being consolidated. But in fact nothing tangible emerged. The discussion steadily became more restricted and more parochial. Television, radio and the newspapers cannot be expected to give coverage to the same subject indefinitely, and other matters claimed their attention. More surprisingly, however, the discussion also died down in the churches. Although Dr Robinson had argued that the most fundamental categories of Christian belief – God, the supernatural, religion – had to go into the melting pot, they seemed intent on keeping something like their old shape. Although Dr Robinson had argued that while his views might seem radical and indeed heretical to many, the one thing of which he felt certain amid all his uncertainties was that he had erred in not being nearly radical enough, in many areas few people seemed ready to go even as far as he had.[3] And if this process was already evident before the end of the 1960s, as we have already seen, towards the end of the 1970s it is becoming even more marked.

As happens so often, fierce argument kept the theological discussion going: indifference, avoidance of the issue, the hope that the whole problem would blow over, a determination to carry on business as usual on the part of the more traditionalist members of the church were all factors in its collapse. The power of the status quo proved too much, even in intellectual matters. The result is that it sometimes seems as though the debate over *Honest to God* might never have taken place. Paradoxically, this was never more the case than in the summer of 1977, while I was correcting the proofs of this book, when the publication of *The Myth of God Incarnate*, a collection of essays by a distinguished group of theologians calling for a restatement of the doctrine of the incarnation, brought the first collection of headlines in the national press to rival those of 1963. Not only was there widespread inability to understand the nature of the argument being put forward (which is discussed in chapters 4 and 5 below), but considerable shock at an approach which in some aspects had its origin as far back as the nineteenth century.

Even ten years ago, there was plenty of evidence of conservatism within the church as a whole, a fondness for clichés and emotive slogans, a tendency to take too much for granted, a complacency about the real needs of modern men and women. But it did look as if the newly emerging force might begin to tip the balance. Ecclesiasticism was being relegated to a secondary position behind a concern for the way things really were, for man's real nature and destiny. People actually talked about God in public. There was a sense that what was being discussed was in the end a matter of life and death, something that made a real difference. The questions asked, and obviously asked with the emotions and from the heart, as well as in an intellectual way, were part of a search for ultimate reality, even if that reality might prove to be unpalatable or devastating. The writers of books and articles may have had difficulty in finding the right language with which to address their newly enlarged readership, but at least they showed an awareness of a significant lay audience which was not primarily concerned for reassuring teaching, correct doctrine, or the defence of traditional positions. This audience even welcomed having its difficulties brought out into the open, although clear answers might be lacking. It was moved and impressed when theologians had the courage to say quite openly, 'I don't know'.

For whatever reasons, these concerns have not only faded from the public domain; they are largely absent from the more restricted area of church discussion as well. The number of new religious books being published is diminishing, and those that do appear are of a very different kind. Dominant among them are those addressed to Christians in the evangelical tradition for whom the questions raised in *Honest to God* seem to cause no problems at all; other titles offer encouragement and helps to prayer and worship in a fairly traditional vein. In fact, there seems to be a mass return to the reading of books along these lines by writers of previous generations, a development which is coupled with a marked decline in creative or good critical religious writing, the exceptions being books of the kind mentioned in the previous chapter. The number of religious newspapers and periodicals in circulation has declined dramatically (*New Christian* had a life of only five years); many have disappeared completely and there is evidence now not only that circulations are falling but that editors are finding it increasingly difficult to include enough good material to fill the available space. Those church newspapers which remain tend on the whole to be comfortable 'house journals', while the specialist monthlies and quarterlies usually remain firmly rooted in their academic world, most of them devoted to tackling small-scale questions in great and learned details. The religious books that are published seem increasingly less likely to be reviewed outside this narrow circle, just as discussion of religious questions in the national press is likely to be trivial or non-existent. From time to time television and radio may devote some space to religious questions, but fundamental matters of belief are rarely tackled in any depth.

The picture has had to be drawn in very broad lines, but there ought to be enough truth in it to hold. What has happened? Where have all the questions and the questioners gone? What are the questioners doing now? Even Dr Robinson himself seems to all intents and purposes to have left the field and to be devoting himself almost exclusively to specialist study of the New Testament, leaving untouched the questions of the wider context of belief in which the New Testament is set. The debate over *Honest to God* may itself have been a fashion, a temporary sensation brought about by a number of chance circumstances. It may have taken place in the middle of what are now being regarded as the 'silly sixties'. But are the undercurrents which could be seen in the debate fashions, too? Was the whole thing a charade and nothing more? One might argue that time and again things went off on the wrong track, that the discussion was better at demolishing ideas than putting together a viable pattern of belief for today, that those involved in it were too often insiders working off their personal frustrations and becoming intoxicated with the excitement of iconoclasm, that it all too quickly left the average person far behind, and much more. This is no place for a detailed historical critique of the episode. But when this has been said, have the questions really been answered one way or the other?

By remaining essentially silent, by refusing to consider radical change, has the church, despite all that has been said in the first chapter, emerged strengthened and triumphant from the ordeal? Is traditional belief and practice still essentially viable? From the point of view of believing and worshipping, at any rate, are those who feel that sense of malaise, dissatisfaction, remoteness from the contemporary church and its preoccupations the ones who are out of step and who need to be brought into line?

Or has our image of God really gone – once and for all? Is the outcome of the *Honest to God* debate a final demonstration that there is no God and that religious belief and practice are an illusion? Is our society at last an essentially secular one, and are people now committed to nothing more than making the most of this world and the material goods it has to offer (or alternatively trying to rescue this world and to preserve its resources) because that is quite simply all that there is?

Has that audience of half believers, who at one time thought that something was going to happen, those rejecting the churches in their present form but still feeling there was something to religious belief, have all these now been reconciled to a less radical way of looking at things? Have they just quietly given up and abandoned the sinking ship? Is there nothing left to talk about?

Any detailed answers to these questions would prove to be very complicated indeed, and would require a great deal of research and a large book of their own. But it is possible to suggest some main outlines. If one is thinking about potential interest in religion and particularly Christianity, as opposed to committed membership of a church or movement, then the most noticeable thing is variety of approach and understanding with an unprecedented degree of tolerance. This of itself would seem to rule out two extremist claims, no matter how pressingly and vociferously they are put.

On the one hand, evangelical Christianity seems to be growing more strongly than ever. Within churches of many traditions there has been a spread of the ethos of this approach with its stress on biblical fundamentalism, personal conversion and individual piety. Anyone from this tradition who has read this book to this point will doubtless have been throwing up his hands at its (to him) despondent and one-sided description. Its language will be completely different from what he knows. It is indeed impossible not to be impressed by the life and the achievements of the evangelicals, not least where Pentecostalism has come to be part of their life. In many places they stand as a challenge to other patterns of Christian faith, as to the disinterested, and the strength of their clear message and their enthusiastic groups and individuals is undeniable. And yet, the exclusivist outlook, the self-assurance and the blindness to so many issues, the very simplicity, make this approach impossible as a satisfying answer.

This is not the place for an extended discussion of the evangelical approach. The difficulty it presents ultimately lies in the way in which it can turn into a form of escapism, rather than engagement with the modern world. And whatever the vigour of the life which it presents, the superficiality of its intellectual position, at times verging on downright dishonesty, and its need for constant special pleading of one sort or another, must be a deterrent to anyone who is given to much reflection. If this approach were characteristic of the future pattern religion needs to take, it seems that the sacrifice we would be asked to make would be to abandon our basic drive to see how *everything* might make sense without irresolvable contradictions. We would have to reconcile ourselves to living in two unrelated worlds held together by an all too capricious deity. And against the background which we have been considering in this chapter, for a great many people this would mean becoming something other than they were and being untrue to what they believe they can see. This is far too high a price to pay, and it cannot justifiably be exacted in the name of the gospel.

On the other hand, it just does not seem to be the case that secular man has now arrived on the scene, the man without a 'God-shaped blank' inside him, the man who has ceased to be concerned with the dimensions of the supernatural and the religious altogether. Even in the time of the debate over *Honest to God* it was becoming evident to many that some of the views of the more outspoken secularists in the discussion were misplaced. If much of the noise was being made by those within the churches who were particularly anxious that certain beliefs and practices should be abolished once and for all, there was no mistaking the quieter voices of those who were not looking primarily for demolition, but for enough to put together to make up a faith which they could honestly embrace. And as time went on, there was a good deal of evidence to suggest that in theory, at any rate, they had more chance of doing this in the second half of the century than they might have had in the first.

To those reading widely, there were signs that the positions of some of the traditional old opponents of religious belief were crumbling. Philosophical attacks on the possibility of belief in God were far less strong than they had been, and the view that philosophical developments from Kant, through Feuerbach to modern linguistic analysis, had made nonsense of talk about God was no longer accepted as self-evident. There were even suggestions that it might be possible to revive the ancient discipline of metaphysics, the philosophy of ultimate reality, and attempts were made at outlines of a new natural theology, at arguments for the existence of God from pointers in the natural world, quite apart from the Christian revelation. Sociologists were more sophisticated in their approach to the phenomena of religious belief, and some even challenged the idea that an irreversible process of secularization, an exclusive concern only with this world, had set in. Science and religion were no longer seen as implacably hostile enemies as they had been since the nineteenth century; it was accepted that the make-up of men and their world was far more complicated than any explanations offered so far. There were other possible views of the psychology of religious belief than those of Freud. Whatever the situation might be in practice, whatever the popular views about religion still held in some areas, those engaged in a search for deepened ways of expressing religious belief for our time did not have to be too disheartened.

Two remarkable non-Christian documents illustrating this trend are worth mentioning briefly. The first is a short tract by Philip Toynbee, entitled *Towards the Holy Spirit*, published in 1973, but embodying thoughts which could be found elsewhere before then, if not put so compellingly and so succinctly. He began a series of more than two hundred brief pensées, assembled to present a cogent argument, by dismissing the traditional positions taken up by Christian doctrine as expressed in historic statements of belief. This was not surprising. It was, however, much more striking that, although not himself a Christian nor even an avowed believer in God, he went on to dismiss the positions that seemed to have been reached by modern scientists and philosophers in scathing terms. Scientists, he argued, should recognize that they had been brought face to face with phenomena which they were able to describe only in terms at least as repulsive to common sense as any that were ever used by Christian theologians. There was room for mystery here, as there also was within philosophy. Modern positivist philosophers, he continued, should recognize that they had not only failed in their declared intention of making linguistic sense of modern scientific discoveries; they had not even been able to solve or to shelve most of the traditional philosophical puzzles.

He then went on to talk in a moving way about the mysteries which were still to be found in human life, being drawn particularly to the evidential value of the life and witness of saints and mystics. Here was a large body of reported experience from the best of all possible human sources, saying that this experience was incomparably the most valuable and the most significant they had ever known. How was this to be fitted into our understanding of reality?

Rejecting a series of arguments which would reduce this sort of experience to something less, Philip Toynbee finally came to the conclusion that over and above us there is a supra-personal force which might be called the Holy Spirit, experienced both as personal and as non-personal, existing outside the natural order and independently of any human or other mind. He ended by saying that it did not seem irrational, superstitious or beyond our means to speak of the Holy Spirit and to pray for its descent on ourselves and on our world. But for this descent it was necessary to be prepared to wait, cultivating love, hope and faith and resisting 'that heat for certainty which seems to be one of our strongest impulses and a principal cause of our most constant errors and afflictions'.[4]

His remarks could be paralleled, in a different way, elsewhere. Peter Brook, the famous theatre producer, remembered above all for his brilliant production of *A Midsummer Night's Dream*, could speak in the same vein, in articles and in his book *The Empty Space*. ('This theatre is holy because its purpose is holy; it has a

24

clearly defined place in the community and it responds to a need the churches can no longer fill.')[5] So could music critics and composers, their words amply confirmed by the growing hold of music on people's lives – and so, too, could a journalist renowned for his acid wit and his skill as a hatchet man.

Bernard Levin, writing at the end of the decade, began his brilliant account of the 1960s, *The Pendulum Years*, with a picture of Britain far removed from Dr Robinson's secular man:

> Teachers, prophets, sibyls, oracles, mystagogues, avatars, haruspices and mullahs roamed the land, gathering flocks about them as easily as holy men in nineteenth-century Russia, and any philosophy, from Zen Buddhism to macrobiotics and from violence as an end in itself to total inactivity as an end in itself, could be sure of a respectful hearing and a group of adherents, however temporary their adherence might prove.[6]

He contrasted the claims of science to mastery over the environment, as presented by Dr Edmund Leach in the Reith Lectures, with the Old Testament-like holocausts of cattle in their hundreds of thousands – the only known way of dealing with foot-and-mouth disease. And he moved on to the popularity of astrology, scientology and sectarian beliefs. It was all tongue-in-cheek, scintillating and constantly amusing, and this vein continued throughout the book. But there is no mistaking a different tone which is all the more impressive when it comes through in this context. As when, after having his fun with the *Honest to God* debate, Levin talked of the bishop's defenders who included, in addition to powerful and eminent thinkers, 'the mute hundreds of thousands who had bought his book and the mute thousands who had written to him (they far outnumbered his critics)'.[7] And even more so later when, having recounted many of the scandals and sensations of the decade, he turned to the arts and devoted a chapter to describing what he called moments when experiences as intense as any art can offer came his way.[8] At this point the language is almost reminiscent of passages in Philip Toynbee's book, going beyond the vocabulary of art and perhaps closer to the vocabulary of religion. For him they took place in the opera house, at performances of Beethoven's *Fidelio*, Richard Strauss's *Die Frau ohne Schatten* and Wagner's *Mastersingers*; for others they may have taken place elsewhere, in theatre or concert hall or art gallery or from the pages of a book: something 'out of this world' in the strictest sense.

It would be wrong to press the point too hard, but it does need to be made. Christian belief is not a 'faith once delivered to the saints', which simply needs to be handed on unchanged in its expression from one generation to another. In a famous phrase, it is rather faith looking for understanding, an attempt to develop a particular perspective on the world which has come into being because of the chain of events which lead up to Jesus Christ and are influenced by the historical impact that he made. In furthering this understanding Christians have always been deeply involved with the cultures of their times. This has happened throughout church history, and hindsight shows us that it has happened even during periods when Christians have vigorously protested that this was not the case.

So in our time too, when Christian writing and teaching so often gives the impression of being ingrown and impoverished, it is important to listen to what is being said by the more sensitive, the more thoughtful, the more eloquent, the more privileged among our society. If they too can at times be brought to the edge of religious experience, be drawn towards religious belief as a moth towards a flame, they may have a contribution to make towards an understanding of how Christianity might be expressed, even if they have no formal allegiance to the churches. Certainly, it is wrong if between them and the life of the churches there should be a gulf and a lack of communication.

There is a feeling abroad in the churches that somehow belief must be expressed in direct, straightforward and assertive ways, a pining for a message which will win back the allegiance of large numbers of the wider public. But there is much in our culture to suggest that this may at best be an idle dream and at worst in effect a longing for a distorted over-simplification. To many thinking people, life and the world now seem so complicated that it seems impossible that there should be any truthful answer.

While this is so, those who look for insights which are more than obvious and trivial will treasure ways of talking about deeper religious issues, of hinting at religious insights.

We have not, in fact, touched so far in this chapter on specifically Christian beliefs. We shall be looking at them more closely in due course. Its aim has been more limited: to show that there have been many signs in recent years that both the truth of Christian faith as we can understand it and the way in which it can best be communicated will probably be found somewhere between the traditional formulations of the past and the more radical statements about secular man and a world without God. Here there may well be a way forward. It is still possible to hope that along it we might find a new pattern of faith by which to live.

But, as we have seen, the intellectual questions are only part of the picture. The mind is only part of our total human make-up. As was clear from the way in which the discussion over *Honest to God* was carried on, we also need a focal point for our emotions, something to satisfy that deep religious longing which is more than purely intellectual. We need somewhere where we can put mind and heart into action, and we need somewhere where we can share and help to realize what we see and hope for and believe with others, before the vision fades and our energies are drained off into the sand. We need somewhere to belong. And that brings us back to the churches.

3

What Happened to the
New Reformation?

Honest to God was far from being an intellectual treatise. One reviewer, asking himself what kind of book it was, concluded that it might best be described as a book of devotion; it was a cri de coeur against tying up our talk about God with outmoded views of the universe which we could no longer make our own, yet at the same time it was passionately concerned with God, in the way that is the mark of a book of devotion. Others saw it as a prophecy, a call to action, a programme for change. And the concluding section of *Honest to God* was concerned precisely with that. What did its statements mean for the future life and shape of the church? Anything that helped to keep the church's frontiers open, Dr Robinson argued, should be strengthened and reformed; anything that turned it in on itself as a religious organization should be suspected and deplored.

Honest to God appeared at a time when there was already discontent with the pattern of life within the churches and when there was already considerable discussion about what might be done. Large numbers of the most able clergy were attracted into movements like Parish and People, the Keble Conference Group, the Renewal Group in Methodism and similar bodies. There was no lack of ideas, from the more conservative side to the radical wing in which the 'non-church' party rivalled the 'God is dead' school. But the strength of the arguments for change, the evidence they could claim in their support and their concern for greater realism are unmistakable. So too was the predominantly optimistic vein in which the discussion was carried on. Parallels were drawn with earlier creative periods of church history, and the phrase which began to emerge again and again was that the church was trembling on the verge of a 'new Reformation'. The phrase was taken up by both critics and supporters of Dr Robinson, and the publication of *Honest to God* was even compared with the famous nailing of Luther's ninety-five theses to the church door at Wittenberg in 1518. *New Christian* emulated him with the same number of its own. Bliss was it in that dawn to be alive . . .

The poetry of Monica Furlong's vision captures the mood at first hand in a way that no prosaic description could:

> Within the strange, sprawling, quarrelling mass of the churches, within their stifling narrowness, their ignorance, their insensitivity, their stupidity, their fear of the senses and of truth, I perceive another Church, one which really is Christ at work in the world. To this Church men seem to be admitted as much by a baptism of the heart as of the body, and they know more of intellectual charity, of vulnerability, of love, of joy, of peace, than most of the rest of us. They have learned to live with few defences and so conquered the isolation which torments us. They do not judge, especially morally; their own relationships make it possible for others to grow. It does not matter what their circumstances are, what their physical and mental limitations are. They really are free men, the prisoners who have been released and who in turn can release others.
>
> There are more people like this in the churches than outsiders ever imagine, and meeting them is never a surprising or unnatural experience, like catching a glimpse of Stylites on his pillar. This, one knows, as soon as one has seen it, has a naturalness about it, a rightness, a sweetness that one would give anything to share. To see it is to know that this is how one ought to be, only somehow it went wrong, and one got lost instead in the muddle of worry and work and people and money.
>
> If the Church could offer this kind of fulfilment to more people it would be doing the work of healing and preaching the gospel which is what it exists to do.[1]

Dr Robinson himself was not so sure. He was sufficiently sceptical to remark that the prospects were that even thicker darkness was likely before any sign of a dawn might begin to break through.[2] Nevertheless, when his next book appeared, in 1965, it took the fashionable and heady phrase as its title, albeit followed by a cautious question mark.

The New Reformation? was essentially a book about the church. By the time it was published the main impetus of the first debate had died down; its readership was very much smaller and its appeal much more parochial. The new book did not, in fact, follow on logically from *Honest to God*, and like *Honest to God*, it failed to question a number of things about which it should have been more critical. So it was not the application of the earlier theological questioning to a specific situation. However, the relationship in mood was plain enough.

The church, Dr Robinson argued, needed a spring clean. It had too many structures, too many fixed assets, rather than too few. A 'stripping of the structures' was called for. The church had the characteristics of the dinosaur and the battleship, saddled with an organization and a programme beyond its means, so that it was constantly involved in problems of supply and preoccupied with survival. Its inertia, moreover, was such that the financial allocations, the legalities, the channels of organization, the attitudes of mind, were all set in the direction of continuing and enhancing the status quo. And anyone who tried to go across these channels in a different direction would exhaust most of his energies before ever getting anywhere at all.

Dr Robinson was realist enough to be aware that such stripping down could not be a sudden process. But change had to be prepared for. It was important to keep in mind goals towards which the church might move. For instance, the church ought to be centred on particular patterns of community rather than historic buildings, perhaps set up in what was now the wrong place. It ought to cut down on routine and administration. Perhaps it should even give away some of its existing endowments. For just as Jesus was to be seen, in the phrase constantly repeated through *Honest to God*, as the 'man for others', so the church had to be seen as the servant which was there for others, not in order to assert its own claims. Above all, it had to become an open community, making contact with those outside and becoming involved rather than keeping its distance.

The crisis in thinking about traditional Christian doctrine became relevant at this point. Much of what was presented as the good news, the gospel, Dr Robinson argued, was in fact meaningless. The important thing was not to try to get people to the churches, even in the metaphorical sense, but to meet them where they were, to begin with the questions they were asking. Or they might be invited to share the experience first and discuss the definitions afterwards. The new theology which was needed should itself be a lay theology, which would consist in reflecting on the new situation which would come about, in which divisions between clergy and laity, professionals and amateurs, men and women, would be broken down and all would be involved together in the new enterprise.

So heady was the discussion of the new form of the church that it might have been expected that change really was just around the corner. And indeed, if the thought of *Honest to God* and *The New Reformation?* had been on the right lines, radical change is what one would have expected. By now, not only should theology have taken on a very different pattern, but the churches should have been transformed out of all recognition, if they had not collapsed in the process. Or, to put it more realistically, institutions being what they are: since churches are institutions and do not change over night, one might have expected at least that the undercurrent of thinking and questioning and criticizing within them would have had more detectable influence. Or, failing even that, one might have expected a great deal more visible tension within the church, a great deal more pressure for radical change and reform than is evidently the case now.

Of course, the situation is not a static one. But the most potent factor is that of economic pressure. The Church of England, at one time apparently in a position to survive to the end of the century with relatively few financial problems, now views even the year 1980 with anxiety and has to think hard about its funding.

31

How can it finance machinery which has grown increasingly expensive, but which shows little signs of being reduced, or how can it spread its dwindling manpower over more and more territory? The jumble sales and the bazaars have to cope with increased demands from the diocese as well as with decaying churches and new boilers. And this process will go on, perhaps having more effect on church life than any amount of discussion about the demands of theology and the outlook of the modern world.

But that is hardly anything to be proud of. We all have to learn to cope with inflation and come to terms with a reduced standard of living. The vision of a new Reformation had something rather different in mind. And in that respect, it does seem as if, rather than leading to a new dawn, the ferment of thought characteristic of the churches in the 1960s has given birth to a new conservatism – and worse.

That might seem surprising in view of what has in fact happened within the churches over the last twenty years. Looking back, in a retrospective article written as recently as January 1977, Dr Robinson commented on the 'fantastic' changes in the church – 'at a speed which it would be difficult to credit, especially in the Church of England, were it not that we have changed with them'.[3]

At this point, however, the irreverent *bon mot* of one of the most clear-sighted of Anglicans rises into one's consciousness: 'It often seems that the Church of England, along with many other churches, is in favour of change as long as it makes no difference.'[4]

The more thoughtful observer of modern developments might feel tempted to agree. A good deal of what looks like change and modernization, he might feel, is in fact essentially conservative. You can indeed make changes in institutions without altering their basic character. Some changes may in fact be little more than cosmetic, elaborate window dressing, papering over the cracks, because the thinking behind them does not go deep enough, does not ask the deepest questions. New forms may emerge, new patterns develop, which at the same time leave the important things essentially the same.

Changes have indeed been made over recent years, but have

they made enough difference? Have the questions asked in fact been deep enough? It might be a reasonable test to look at some of the areas which have been singled out as indicating progress and to ask precisely what has been achieved. The examples I have chosen mostly come from the life of the Church of England, since that is the church about which I know most and to which I belong, but there is no compelling reason to think that they are unique. Before we come to them, however, one preliminary point needs to be made. Whatever the change, it has been presided over by the Convocations and Church Assembly of the Church of England (later to become General Synod), which has laid down official guidelines for new developments which it expects to be obeyed. And one crucial issue which demands far more consideration than it has yet been given is whether any single form of government, let alone that which the Church of England in fact has, is capable of directing change in so difficult and pluralist a context.

The way in which the official church government has gone about its business has not been encouraging. Its chief preoccupation after the Second World War was a revision of its Canon Law (dictionary definition: 'The body of ecclesiastical rules or laws imposed by authority in matters of faith, morals and discipline'). Six years after the publication of *Honest to God* the work was finally complete, having taken up a vast amount of time and energy. Shuttled to and fro for discussion and revision, 112 canons were laboriously prepared, so that in 1963, while in the world at large Christians were agonizing how it was possible even to think of God or to pray to him, preparations were being made to give definitive instruction to members of the Church of England, in Trevor Beeson's words, 'that a man might not marry his mother or his daughter, that the clergy should prepare for Confirmation any who desired to be Confirmed, that a copy of the Book of Common Prayer must be kept in every church and that the apparel of the clergy should be suitable to their office, save for purposes of recreation and other justifiable reasons'.[5]

It is easy to laugh at General Synod, and those involved in it might well feel inclined to argue that any church, particularly a national, established church, needs a properly regulated form of government. But any body which meets far less frequently than Parliament, and with far fewer financial resources at its disposal, needs to think extremely carefully how its time is allocated. It also needs to be sure that it is representative of the church over which it is set.

Here there are two obvious problems. First of all, the demands which General Synod makes on the time of its members restricts the number of people, particularly lay people, who feel able to offer themselves for election. Apart from the full-time clergy, membership is inevitably made up largely of those lay people who have sufficient leisure or freedom and financial independence to take part, and these will inevitably colour the debates held and the decisions made. The existence of synods at lower levels, the diocese and the deanery, are intended to provide a link with the wider church. But here again there are the same kind of problems, together with the discouraging combination of petty bickering and soul-destroying boredom which seems to have become so much the hallmark of synodical discussion. No one who has sat for hours in the public gallery while General Synod has been in session, or has been a representative at a less exalted synod, can have come away feeling that here he or she has seen the church at anything like its best. And so for one reason or another the best and most able members are debarred or deterred from taking a more active part and the position becomes worse.

A contributory factor here is the second problem, that within the synods at all levels there has been no resolution of the question of power. With its fundamental structure of forty-three dioceses, each under the autonomous control of a bishop and not necessarily committed to a single line of policy, and presided over by an Archbishop of Canterbury whose powers are not as great as might appear at first sight, the Church of England in any case looks like an organization designed to resist the possibility of all change. Given this underlying position, there is no chance of the more local synods having really effective power without either the voluntary abrogation of their authority by the bishops or widespread reform. Synods can discuss and advise to their heart's delight, but in the end of the day the power does not in fact lie with them. Theology and democracy make uneasy partners, and the tensions between them have yet to be resolved.

This raises the whole question of the nature of authority in matters of religious belief and practice. There is clearly considerable dissatisfaction both about and within the present system, for all the attention that has been devoted to it. Given the terms of reference and the limits of what is possible, it might be argued that the best has been made of an insoluble task – but does that not perhaps mean that the issues involved should have been approached in a different way?

Had this happened, in the Church of England and elsewhere, the position over church unity might have been much more satisfactory. Here, it is claimed, there have certainly been great changes – but what do they amount to?

The Week of Prayer for Christian Unity in January 1977 was marked by considerable publicity for an agreed joint statement by representatives of the Anglican and Roman Catholic churches on the ministry of a kind which would have been thought impossible a short while ago, while a Joint Working Party for Christian Union at the same time announced plans for the member churches (most of the major traditions) to 'covenant' together to seek union by a particular date (which was not in fact specified).

These statements might have been thought to be landmarks, but they were greeted with little enthusiasm, and seem to have become as ephemeral as the rest of the news of the time. The trouble with them was the question of their representativeness and the language in which they were expressed.

For whom, it was asked, were the statements speaking? What body of opinion did they represent? How did they relate to views held in the local churches?

The General Synod of the Church of England is an illustration of the problem of representing local thinking within a wide-ranging church in a governing body. But the problem goes even deeper than that. As has been said, time and again, one of the reasons why church union is such a complex subject is that it is necessary to take into account the fact that divisions are no longer denominational, between say Methodists and Orthodox, Baptists and Roman Catholics. As well as being vertical, in this way, they are also horizontal, so that certain groups (teachers, students, theologians, for example) may find that they may have more in common across the different traditions than they have with other members of the same tradition. Their churches may be separated by official differences, but in the new climate of thinking and understanding these differences no longer seem to be differences about what may be the truth and what may not be, which is how they arose: rather, the whole question is one of discipline and obedience. It seems to them that official regulations, rather than convictions which can be given rational justification, are what gets in the way.

This explains the strange twofold reaction to the fiasco of the rejection of the proposals for unity between Anglicans and Methodists by General Synod in 1970, despite the overwhelming desire for closer links between the two churches, on a vote which in any other representative assembly would in fact have carried the day for union. On the one hand it was taken very seriously, and at the time of the collapse of the plans there was no lack of suggestion, even from quite serious churchmen, that the official position should be ignored and that as much should be done as possible at a local level to further mutual co-operation between the members of the two churches, almost by way of protest. On the other, a view developed that the proposals were less important than they had seemed and that the way forward lay on quite different lines, because the type of thinking on which they were based was irrelevant.

We shall have to consider at length, in the next chapter, the question of the language in which the agreed statements between churches have been expressed. For the moment, it need only be pointed out that it is very far removed indeed from everyday speech and is far too vague to have much practical significance. It is all very well, for example, for Anglicans and Roman Catholics to have agreed that they can affirm together that 'The sacramental body and blood of the Saviour are present as an offering to the believer awaiting his welcome. When this offering is met by faith, a life-giving encounter results. Through faith Christ's presence becomes no longer just a presence *for* the believer, but also a presence *with* him.'[6] But what does this mean?

Church unity is one of the areas in which rapid change is said to have taken place, but the indications here are that some of the most important issues are only on the verge of being raised. The question of meaning brings us on to a second area of change, that of public worship. The Book of Common Prayer in the Church of England, not long ago the only book used in public worship, has almost been abandoned and there are plans for it to be replaced by a completely new book in 1980. A first series of new services ranging from the eucharist to confirmation, marriage and burial, and for some Anglican reason known as Series 2, has now given way to a Series 3. 'You' has taken the place of 'Thou' as a form of address to God, the creeds and the old canticles of praise have been newly translated, and prayers have been modernized or rewritten. All the old hymn books have been given new supplements, and new hymn books have been compiled, new settings for the services written. The way in which the eucharist is celebrated has changed, with the celebrant facing the people. And what has happened in the Church of England has happened in other churches as well. The Methodist Church prides itself on its new service book, and the Roman Catholic Church, where the speed of the transition from Latin to the vernacular and the relaxation of liturgical style are especially notable, is the most striking instance of all. This does represent remarkable change, and often change for the good. But, once more, it is change within a limited framework, and alongside the approval and the appreciation there is also dissatisfaction.

One compelling recent discussion has pointed out how the rapid change in public worship has, in the Church of England at any rate, been followed in many quarters by equally rapid disappointment, if not disillusion. At least there is a sense of unease and anti-climax, a feeling that all is not as it should be. 'People do not enjoy going to church as much as once they did.'[7] Once again, the reason may well be that the change is misguided and that the thought has not been deep enough, leaving the situation too much the same, for all the appearance of new developments.

As has already been pointed out, the meaning of the eucharist and indeed of much of the language in which it is celebrated is still too obscure. Putting old concepts into modern word-forms is not enough. And it is only necessary to look at the new forms of service to see that whatever the principles behind their construction, and the new knowledge that they claim to represent, they are backward-looking rather than forward-looking, conservative rather than radical. They may reflect the newest findings of liturgical scholarship, but they do not even begin to grapple with the question of what a liturgy for our time should be. They neither come to grips with the reflections on Christian doctrine and traditionalist ideas which were expressed in the discussion over *Honest to God*, nor do they have about them the all-important sense of poetry, the evocative capacity for bringing glimpses of God, which was in fact conveyed in the older services and which is still an important part of Christian worship.

Those with eyes to see are made all too aware that the present wording and structure of the Anglican services are often the result of their passage to and from General Synod: is it just a coincidence that the best prayer in the Series 3 eucharist, 'Father of all', comes right at the end and was spared being subjected to this process in so rigorous a way?

Nowhere is the attempt at rigorous control by Synod made more clear than in the regulations for worship. While the situation of the churches would seem to cry out for a more pluralistic approach, uniformity enforced by a central authority takes the place of variety and the opportunity for local experiment. There is not even any official guidance which would encourage local explorations into the meaning of worship, though there is much to be said for a kind of two-tier system, in which informal groups might worship with greater freedom and in so doing learn lessons which in due course might benefit the whole church.

Above all, recent developments in public worship have produced a new and narrow domination of liturgy by the Bible. It is assumed without further ado that liturgy simply is a catena of biblical texts, with the result that the two important focal points for the Christian are made to be the words of the Bible and the particular act of worship, to the exclusion of the wealth of thought that has come in between. This gives the Bible a place out of all proportion to what might seem to be its role in public worship on the basis of a more balanced understanding.

And so we come to yet another area where it might be argued that considerable change has taken place. Surely, it will be argued, there is great significance in the way in which the Bible has been retranslated in so many different ways. The Authorized Version, dominant less than a generation ago, has given place to countless new translations, most of them very recent indeed. Millions upon millions of new translations of the Bible have been sold: *The Jerusalem Bible* (1966), *The New English Bible* (completed 1970), *The Living Bible* (1973) and the *Good News Bible* (completed 1976) have all made their mark and have been the subject of considerable publicity, and there are more new versions on the way.

That evidence certainly cannot be denied. But who has bought all those millions of copies of the Bible? What actual effect have they had? Is there any sign that as a result there has been any change, any greater understanding and knowledge of what the Bible actually says? The evidence from most congregations, the pupils in the majority of schools and those who give answers to television or radio quiz programmes is that despite this great increase of versions, knowledge of the Bible is certainly not growing. In many cases ignorance seems greater than it was before. Nor is this a phenomenon limited to Great Britain. An American author wrote a book entitled *The Strange Silence of the Bible in the Church*, the basic argument of which was that despite a century of intensive biblical scholarship, despite a vast amount of literature about the Bible as well as the new translations, many preachers find it less and less easy to use the Bible in sermons, Bible study groups find it more and more difficult to function, and the lack of knowledge of even the most basic parts of the Bible is almost unbelievable.[8]

Within the church, it would be optimistic to say that even the understanding that each of the gospels was written by a different author with a distinct theological perspective within which he selected and arranged the words and actions of Jesus, the idea of Matthew, Mark, Luke and John as four portraits, had penetrated very far. That the gospel accounts may not be taken apart and then harmonized into a single narrative may be commonplace knowledge to the student of the New Testament; it is not to the average congregation, who are still quite likely to have their Good Friday devotions arranged round such a composite picture of 'the seven last words from the cross'. One of the basic tools for understanding precisely how the four gospels convey knowledge of the life of Jesus is the synopsis, a book containing the gospel texts set in parallel columns, so that it is possible to trace the relationships between them; merely to look at such a book without any other helps whatsoever is illuminating and prompts a whole series of important questions. But such a basic handbook is extremely rare and is seldom found outside the circle of university teachers and students, say on a parish priest's desk, let alone in the possession of members of the congregation. How can anyone be said to take the gospels seriously if they do not even begin to read them thoroughly?

By all appearances the Bible is predominantly used so to speak as background music, rather than being listened to with close attention to the score, its construction and the various forms that make it up. Or it is quarried for proof texts or isolated statements which are then used indiscriminately, without much attention to their context, on the basis of all kinds of unclarified presuppositions. Or it is treasured for its purple passages. It is expected to be of instant use, immediate relevance, without much regard to what it might be saying in its own right and in its own place.

Problems of understanding the Bible are accentuated by the pattern of its use in the contexts where it is most prominent, in public worship or private devotion. Rather than being introduced to the Bible in a rational way, being helped to explore it, church congregations tend to suffer extremes, being over-exposed to some parts, bored to tears by others which are incomprehensible in their liturgical setting (even in the new lectionaries) and expected to understand its significance without ever really being told much about it. There is no encouragement to ask questions, to explore, to appreciate, in the way that other literature, painting or music might be appreciated. On the contrary, much use of the Bible is not far from a kind of mindless brain-washing. And the dead hand of dogmatism is never far away. This is a situation which the new translations, whatever their merits, have done depressingly little to change.

Church order, church unity, public worship, the Bible: whatever the achievements in this area, real changes and convincing solutions still seem a very long way away. The new Reformation has not arrived. And a point made in the first chapter once again comes into the forefront. It is not as though the problem of the churches is that they consist of isolated communities of people, defending unfashionable but true beliefs against a hostile world, striving to live up to certain distinct principles. The obstacle presented by them and to them is not the demanding character of their message. Within them is at least an incipient recognition of the need for some sort of change, coupled with an inability to do much to put really radical change into effect. The desire for change is linked to the desire not to make any difference. All these are classic symptoms not only of spiritual and social malaise but also of intellectual insecurity. There would seem to be a need to probe much deeper and to ask more pressing questions. This means that we must look once again at the very foundations of Christianity, and particularly at the doctrines which gave the church its form and the language in which these doctrines have been traditionally expressed.

4

Beyond Belief?

Doctrine is the major factor in shaping the life of the churches and must therefore be seen as an important cause of their present sorry state. Doctrine dominates their organized life and is the reason why the churches continue in their separate and often warring denominations. Churches are not just Anglican and Baptist, Methodist and Roman Catholic; they are high or low, conservative or evangelical. There are clear dividing lines between those who differ over the nature of the sacrament of the eucharist, the way in which forgiveness of our sins has been achieved, the necessary qualifications for the ordination of clergy, and so on.

It often seems that to some people these issues matter more than anything else in the world – certainly they take up a great deal of time and energy, yet for those who look on the discussions and the arguments from outside they have an air of utter ir-relevance and are carried on in a language and on the basis of presuppositions which seem to have no connection at all with the world in which we now live and the way in which we look at it.

Doctrine is still argued over and taken very seriously. But it is treated in this way only by a minority, concerned that what has been taken over from the past may be forfeited, that by losing its old familiar doctrinal landmarks, expressed in traditional ideas and language, the church may somehow cease to be the church and lose the very ground of its existence.

But do we really need the doctrines that have come down to us in the form in which they are still expressed? Are they not quite as much an encumbrance to the churches as the old buildings and the inefficient organization and all the other depressing features we have been considering in the previous chapters? Is it not time that the beliefs of the churches were expressed in a more comprehensible form? As it is, the old language, as we have seen, either puzzles by its incomprehensibility, offends by making statements which thinking people rightly reject, or simply flows over the heads of somnolent church congregations who have been conditioned into accepting it as part of the paraphernalia of church worship.

It is still an all too common assumption in church circles that whether the world understands the faith or not, whether Christians understand it or not, at any rate Christians believe it and the world does not. This is a very questionable assumption. If the majority of clergy knew what their people actually believed, they could never preach as they do. They would not produce arguments to defend or attack notions that have never entered the heads of the men and women in front of them. They would not exhort people to behaviour in accordance with tenets which their congregations simply ignore. The average English churchgoer believes just as much as he or she can swallow as not improbable, namely, that there is Someone or Something behind it all, that Jesus was a good man, and that the betting on survival after death is evens. These are not the vestiges of Christianity lingering in the dwellers on the housing estate, who have never been near a church since they were sent once or twice to Sunday School. This, at bottom, is what a large proportion of regular worshippers would sincerely uphold if pressed.[1]

The words do not come from some radical attack on the church and its members from one of its enemies. They appear, in fact, in one of the more positive books about Christianity written in the last decade. And they would seem to be true. At any rate, he would be a bold man, or fortunate indeed in his experience, who set out to challenge them. And if they are in fact true, they are one more indication of a very sick church.

Yet how can things be otherwise, given the accepted pattern of teaching and learning in the church? For the church's direct involvement in teaching at all levels is minimal: with the decline in Sunday schools, the most that the average church member is likely to learn is at confirmation classes, through sermons and – if he or she is particularly diligent – at the occasional study group, while all the time the traditional pattern of church worship and preaching goes on, largely beyond understanding, and governed by principles which are never stated explicitly and would probably arouse amazement if they were.

If doctrine were different, the churches might be different, for concerted thought about the nature of the church, of Christian belief and of the characteristics of a Christian way of life might show a need for a change of priorities. Some of the concerns and activities which are now thought most important might fade into the background, and others might be seen as calling for top priority action. So it is to doctrine that we must now turn. Indeed, without serious attention to restating its beliefs, the church runs the risk of losing all intellectual credibility and power of effective action.

But how can Christian doctrine change without Christianity ceasing to be Christianity? What happens if you challenge what are held to be the essentials of Christian faith: belief in God the Father, the incarnation and the saving work of Jesus Christ his Son, the presence of the Holy Spirit in the church and the sacraments, and through them in the Christian believer? Perhaps one of the reasons why more questions are not asked is the fear of the consequences that might result.

The fear is an understandable one – but is no excuse for not asking questions, particularly when the present situation seems so unsatisfactory. Nor need the result necessarily be destructive. A century or so ago scholars began asking new questions about the Bible and in so doing caused a panic in the churches. Experience has proved that their work has enriched, rather than destroyed, our knowledge. There is no reason why asking questions about doctrine should not have a similar effect. And because the questions raised by the study of the Bible and the study of doctrine are so similar, it may be helpful to approach the question 'what is doctrine?' by reminding ourselves of the issues involved in asking 'what is the Bible?' This will have the further advantage that at the end of our brief investigation we shall be able to consider what ought to be the new place not only of doctrine, but of the Bible in the church, for that too presents great problems.

We would not have to talk in this way about the Bible and the key elements of Christian doctrine if we could be sure that they were in some demonstrable way removed from the processes of historical change and had a distinct, certainly identifiable validity of their own, unchanging through every age; in other words, if we could be sure that they were an authoritative divine revelation. But being as aware as we are of the way in which history brings change, in ideas, in language, in culture, in knowledge, and knowing that everything – religious and philosophical systems, legal codes and moral principles, the social development of people in different ages – is conditioned by the historical circumstances in which it arose, we find our greatest problem here. All the documents of Christian faith, from the Bible onwards, seem to be what we can be sure that they are: the product of the thought and experience of certain people living at certain times in history and expressed for and in the thought-world of those times.

As soon as we begin to investigate the Bible and its origin we see how true this is. Although scholars still have their arguments, after more than a century of their detailed and wide-ranging research a generally agreed picture is beginning to emerge. There are countless books which tell the story of this scholarly study, and its methods and approach have been brought to life in even more vivid form in programmes like the recent television series *BC – The Archaeology of the Bible Lands*. In effect, a new world has been discovered. By visiting the scenes of events in the Bible, excavating the ruins of cities and discovering artifacts and even documents, archaeologists have been able to reconstruct in some detail the nature of past civilizations and cultures. We now have some idea of what it was like to live in Mesopotamia or Egypt, Palestine or Syria; even of what people thought and how they worshipped. Of course our knowledge is fragmentary, and there are puzzles; but we do have a background, and into this background the Bible can readily be fitted. If it is read in the new perspectives which archaeological discovery provides, it can suddenly emerge in a new light. Abraham and Moses, David and Jeremiah, are no longer figures whose characters can only be filled out from the imagination of the preacher projecting back his own religious ideas and feelings on to the account in the Bible because there is nothing else to go by. Alongside the portraits made familiar by legend and tradition, stories and stained-glass windows, we now have to put the results and the consequences of explorations into a real, past world which will often produce tension and conflict. Figures like Abraham and Moses, in particular, may prove to have far more ingredients in their make-up than appears at first sight, of such complexity that their portraits may even begin to disintegrate under the tensions. For in his exploration the historian cannot just accept what the Bible says in its own terms; he has to try to understand it, which means following the process by which the portraits – and other stories and beliefs – have come into being; and because in many cases his knowledge will be greater than that of tradition and even of those who produced the biblical accounts, his answers will be different from theirs.

Often historians are thought of as trying to prove the Bible right or wrong – but that is not their purpose. Once it is accepted, as we have seen that it must be, that the Bible is the product of a different age, the question does not arise in that form in so simple a way. In terms of the historian's exploration, the Bible belongs to its time and we belong to ours. Therefore he will be trying to think himself back, out of his own attitudes, into the terms of the period with which he is concerned, to understand the mentality of that age. This is, of course, extremely difficult to do. But it can be achieved with some degree of adequacy, and it is possible to imagine what it might have been like in Jerusalem during the reign of David or in Palestine in the time of Jesus, however blurred the scene may be. More than that, the historian can also begin to say, 'Now I see why they thought of God like that, worshipped him in that particular way, observed these particular laws.' And with this perspective most of the old arguments about the morality and crudity of the Old Testament disappear. People are assessed in the terms of their own time, not of ours.

But all this activity takes the historian – and us – back into the past and leaves us there. By their reconstructions, television programmes like *BC* or books about the historical background to the Bible invite us to go on a visit to the period they are dealing with, to learn about situations from another age – and leave us there. They are not concerned with journeying back to our own times, in other words with the question of the relevance that that past might have for us now. There is no giving of a direct message from the past for the present, no indication of the place that the Bible might have for the church for today, in public worship or in private devotion or in deciding ethical questions (and here we can see the first hints of the revolution that might be being called for). It is of the essence of the historian's work that he is true to the past as the past, in its own terms; the moment he tries to make the past a lesson for our time, he risks ceasing to be a historian and becoming a propagandist instead; instead of taking us back into the past for authentic knowledge of how things were, he would take us into one fantasy dreamland or another, introduce us to one fantasy figure or another, simply by reading past evidence through the distorting spectacles of particular present concerns.

For the historian, then, the Bible belongs to the past and must be seen against the background of its own time. The same – and here we reach a much more critical point – is also the case with the person of Jesus, and it is here that we can see most clearly what happens if the historian stops being a historian and tries to relate Jesus more directly to the present.

It is hard not to believe that Jesus is not a figure for all times and that we in fact know very little indeed about him, so great is the attraction exercised by his portrait in Christianity and even outside, and so vivid have been some of the presentations of his life and work. Men have long read the New Testament and he has come alive for them; others have been inspired to write books about him, and what was once attempted in books now appears on radio and television and in the cinema: Dorothy L. Sayers' *The Man Born to be King*; Pier Paolo Pasolini's *The Gospel according to Saint Matthew*; Dennis Potter's *Son of Man*; Franco Zeffirelli's *Jesus of Nazareth* are some recent examples. Views of the artistic merits of these portrayals may vary, but simply by their existence they reinforce the popular conviction that there is an agreed – and true – story to be told. Yet it is here that the historians have their most devastating argument to press, showing convincingly that these presentations of Jesus which are so admired and are found so compelling, are not, and simply cannot be, accounts of Jesus as he was.

The argument was put most vividly by Albert Schweitzer, the brilliant theologian, musician and doctor, who left what could have been a wonderful academic career to work in a hospital at Lambarene, in tropical Africa. Schweitzer read hundreds of books written by nineteenth-century scholars who had attempted to describe Jesus as he really was. Then, in *The Quest of the Historical Jesus*, first published in Germany in 1906, he described what he saw. His lesson is crystal clear. Although the portraits of Jesus are all based on essentially the same material, they differ quite dramatically, and what emerges from them is not so much a portrait of Jesus as he was, as the idea of the highest hopes and values of men of the nineteenth century, projecting these hopes and values back on to 'the founder of Christianity'. 'It was not only each epoch that found its reflection in Jesus,' Schweitzer wrote, 'each individual created him in accordance with his own character.' [2]

This process still goes on: each generation focuses the ideals it feels to be most important on to Jesus. In the most recent past, at the time of *Honest to God*, as we saw, the chosen picture of Jesus was Jesus 'the man for others', 'the one in whom Love has completely taken over, the one who is utterly open to, and united with, the Ground of his being'. [3] But that language already sounds dated to sensitive ears. Since the 1960s our world has grown more violent, our horizons even wider, and so talk of this kind has given way in many areas to yet another picture – Jesus the revolutionary. Schweitzer's book ended at the turn of the last century; it would not be difficult to continue it, writing chapters to bring it down to our own day. An American, John H. Hayes, has in fact collected together some more recent interpretations of Jesus in a book whose title speaks for itself: *Son of God to Superstar*.[4]

The figure of Jesus still has a compelling power. But this may be a power which misleads, if the figure of Jesus is a distortion. The very variety of portraits itself presses home the question 'Who is this Jesus?' All the emphases, all the details cannot be right. And so we are left with the question: how much of his figure is historical and how much of what we imagine is simply a projection of dreams and wishes and hopes on to a name which has been carried round the world over two thousand years by faith and force, prayer and propaganda, until it is embedded deep in our culture and our consciousness? Not just in our own time, but in the past, it has been possible to challenge the church of Jesus in the name of Jesus – two different portraits of the Christ not only diverging, but at war.

In the famous ending to his book, Albert Schweitzer remarked how he came to us 'as one unknown'. Scholars will continue to discuss the degree of our ignorance, but of one thing we can be certain: to see him as as he was it is necessary to see him as a man of his age, not of ours, to whom we must go in his time. And once there, we shall be faced with the same problem: just how can a man of that age mean anything for ours?

It is only necessary to read the gospels straight through, out of a church setting, with the eyes of a historian and with the help of scholars, to see how this must be so. Read *all* the gospels, and not just the familiar passages, and the problems emerge. The teaching of Jesus, for all its greatness, is presented in a form which is conditioned by his background and his age. Some of his sayings are no more than riddles, and because they are handed down in isolation, we may never know what they mean. A remark like that translated, 'From the days of John the Baptist until now the kingdom of heaven has suffered violence and men of violence take it by force' (Matthew 11.12), for instance, is quite incomprehensible. Even familiar words may not have meant quite what they seem to say. Scholars confess puzzlement over the precise meaning of such well-known words as the petition in the Lord's Prayer, 'Give us this day our daily bread' (because the word for 'daily' in the Greek which has come down to us could in fact mean something different). The sum total of his message is something that scholars are still able, quite justifiably, to argue over. 'What did Jesus mean by Son of Man?', 'What is the meaning of the Kingdom of God in Jesus' teaching?', 'Did Jesus foresee his death, and if so what significance did he attach to it?' These are all essay subjects which university theological students are invited to tackle in their initial study of the gospels, and a reading of the evidence alone soon shows them what problems they are up against.

To discuss why the story of Jesus, his teaching and actions, his death and resurrection, have come down to us in apparently so enigmatic and fragmentary a form, and what they mean, would need another book. We have been taking them here only as one specific instance of the way in which, as we look at the Bible and Jesus as they seem to have been, we are drawn back into their own time and their own terms. The Bible is a book from the ancient world and Jesus is a figure from the first century AD and, left to ourselves with our modern cast of mind, without any preconceptions imposed upon us by the churches and their different way of approaching things, that is how we would most naturally go about trying to understand them. And we would come away from such an attempt at understanding with our knowledge enriched.[5]

But now come the anxious questions. Are the Bible and Jesus not more? Is not the Bible the Word of God and is not Jesus the Son of God? After all, this is what Christians have believed down the ages and what many people think to be the very foundation of Christianity. Are we not on the verge of questioning the whole truth of Christian belief?

However, there is a counter-question to be put here. Who says so? Who says that the Bible is the Word of God and that Jesus is the Son of God, and on what grounds? And here, alongside the Bible, our understanding illuminated to some degree by the way in which we have looked at its contents, we come to consider the nature of Christian doctrine.

Christian doctrine, like the Bible, is the product of the thinking and experience of the men of a particular time. It is the attempt of those who came after Jesus and became members of the church to express the meaning of his life, death and resurrection, and in the light of that, to understand the nature of God and the world. It is the attempt of those with faith to achieve understanding.

The period over which Christian doctrine was formed is as varied as the period which saw the making of the Bible, and covered very different cultures and languages. Jesus presumably spoke in Aramaic and spent most of his life in the country areas of Palestine, his ideas formed by the Judaism of his time, however much he broke away from it. By the time of Paul Christianity was still dominated by Judaism, but was now firmly rooted in the Greek-speaking world; the influence of Greek thought increased as the early Christian fathers used Greek philosophy to interpret the gospel. While they were working out their interpretations, Christianity changed from being the religion of a small and comparatively insignificant group to being the official faith of the Roman empire, and when that empire collapsed, Christianity became the dominant factor in the transition from the dark ages to the Renaissance and the Reformation.

Christian doctrine was an attempt to express the meaning of Jesus. To begin with, people had met him, heard him, witnessed his actions, seen him die, believed that they had tangible evidence of his resurrection, and felt that through him a new power had entered their life. They had to explain to themselves and to others what all this meant. So in the categories of thought available to them in their time, they tried to present some sort of interpretation of the evidence. This process of interpretation went on over a period of centuries, as Christians continually tried to find a method which they found satisfactory. Sometimes what was said was rejected because it seemed to say too much; sometimes it was rejected because it did not say enough. Always, there was argument. And there was also change. As the culture of Christians and their background changed, in the way that I have briefly outlined above, so the terms of reference of doctrine changed. New ideas might emerge, as when the whole framework of vivid, pictorial, Jewish thought in terms of parable and simile and 'kingdom of God' and 'Son of Man' gave way to the philosophical abstractions of 'nature' and 'person' and 'substance'; and even terms which remained the same might in fact come to bear very different meanings in their new context. For example, 'Son of God' in the New Testament, where 'son of' can simply be an expression meaning 'like' (as in the case of the disciples who were 'sons of thunder' – compare the modern American 'son of a gun' or 'sonofabitch'), has quite a different meaning there from 'Son of God' in the context of a doctrine of the Trinity like that which we find expressed in the familiar Nicene Creed.

Every now and then, the church would say, 'that's it!', and officially recognized formulations of doctrine would emerge: the Apostles' Creed, the Nicene Creed, the Definition of the Council of Chalcedon in 451 and so on. But as we have seen, these were all statements of their time, expressed in the language of their time, and are as much historically conditioned and timebound as the message of Jesus and the content of the Bible, which we were considering earlier.

Perhaps that is harder to grasp because the creeds in which Christian doctrine is enshrined are presented as statements about how the world is, how God is, eternally, and not as statements about particular events in the past (apart, that is, from their references to Jesus). They have a static, timeless quality to them. But they are none the less statements of their time, for all that. The way in which they look at the world is not our way, and the way in which they think of God is not our way, though it may have been the best way of expressing the meaning of Jesus available to that time. And what can be said of the Christian doctrine of the classical period of the Fathers of the early church (up to, say, the fifth century when the all-important Council of Chalcedon took place) also applies to the methods of formulating doctrine which have been used in the churches ever since, down to the modern period with the rise of historical consciousness.

And here we come to the crux of the matter. For this all too brief discussion of the way in which we might attempt to make sense for our own time of the Bible, of Jesus, of Christian doctrine, points in each case to the same basic question. How do we make use of the past in terms of the present? How can the past speak to us meaningfully in our own very different age? The trouble with the church seems to be that it expects the use of the Bible as a document with a direct message for us today to be effective without very much further thought; that it expects the Jesus of the first century to speak directly to the world of our time; that it expects Christian doctrine hammered out in the period before the scientific revolution to express the essential truth of our mysterious universe. And it gets very worried indeed if anyone hints that this is not the case.

Yet it has presented no satisfactory and clearly understandable explanation of its own, letting this whole intellectual question slide as though with luck it might just go away. But it has not gone, and instead we find ourselves with the mystification which the earlier part of this book has described. The tradition has been taken over and continued simply because it is there and because it is the least form of resistance, despite the fact that the language in which it is expressed is found to be increasingly foreign.

'I have made a decision for Jesus Christ as my Lord and Saviour', 'I believe that Jesus is the Son of God', 'begotten, not made, one in Being with the Father, Through him all things were made'. There are still those who are quite at home using these terms and see no difficulty in them. They may well be shocked and find it incredible that others genuinely do not see what the words in fact mean, repeating them ever more loudly, certain like the proverbial Englishman abroad that if they shout the natives are certain to understand. Whereas our historian will not be puzzled by the fact that to use them in a modern setting causes perplexity: the way in which they can be alien has a parallel in the way in which people would be puzzled if one were to talk about ill-health in terms of humours, of chemical changes brought about by the astronomer's stone or about the sun going round the earth.

The historian can help us to understand the past by recreating it and enabling us to go there and seeing how the legacy which it has handed down to us came into being. He can explain the way in which the Bible and Christian doctrine came into being and he

53

can help to show what we may or may not say that we know about Jesus. He can explain, and we can understand, without any special abstruse and technical language, because that is the way that we are made. The kind of explanations that we understand are especially historical ones. We are no longer capable of thinking of things in terms of what they are. This is the great new development which marks us off from the past.

We can understand, for example, Aquinas or St Paul, but we cannot argue with them. Let St Thomas ask us to define anything – for example the natural law – let him ask us to tell him what it is. We cannot do it. But, given time enough we can relate for him its history. We can tell him what varied forms the natural law has assumed up till now. Historical-mindedness is so much a preconception of modern thought that we can identify a particular thing only by pointing to the various things it successively was before it became the thing which it will presently cease to be.[6]

And if anyone thinks that the statement is exaggerated – go to the studies in modern theology, of doctrines, of institutions like the ministry and the eucharist, the church, the Bible: they will have a good deal to say along these historical lines, about origin and development, but when it comes to discussing what all these things actually *are*, they will fall silent.

This consciousness of historical change is a relatively new element in man's make up, and has come about from our new way of looking at things gained through science and its application to the past. As we know all too well, science has increased our knowledge and power to an incredible degree. There is no need even to illustrate the results of applied science and technology in terms of travel, communication, investigation of the natural world and the power to change it. We are all aware of that. But in addition, the great scientific revolution has transformed not only our knowledge of the past but our whole approach to it. As we have seen, the resources of science, coupled with man's curiosity, imagination and ingenuity, have given us more knowledge of the past than any generation has had before us, and this increased knowledge has changed for all of us, and not just for the specialist, the way we look at things. The greater detailed information we have acquired, along with our greater imaginativeness in asking questions, has led us to see that the men of the past are not just ourselves dressed up in different clothes; they are people who thought differently, lived differently and saw the world differently. More than this, all these different ways of thinking, acting and living hung together, for men of a particular period of culture, in a way that made sense to them, a coherent system.

We have seen how to go about understanding some of those systems of the past, travelling back in time to share with men of that period a different view of the world. We have also seen that such an exploration may widen our own horizons. Just as a person who goes to visit some new country, who makes new friends, who embarks on some completely new hobby or occupation, may find himself and his whole way of looking at life changed as a result, may find a new and deeper perspective, so those who have learned to share in the past may find a deeper wonder at the complex mystery of Christian life and belief. What is opened up here is not just one more crisis: it is a new opportunity for insight and appreciation.[7]

But it prompts questions and it breeds dissatisfaction. Understanding the way people did things in the past is not the same thing as accepting the results of their conclusions as the truth for us today. We can see how people of the Bible thought. But did they always get it right? We can see the terms in which people assessed the meaning and significance of Jesus. But did they always get it right? We can trace out the development of Christian doctrine. But did it always turn out in the right way? And above all, if the process of understanding and interpretation is an on-going one, which involves constant change, can it be a sign of health that we should seek to call an arbitrary halt at various points: the Bible, Jesus, the creeds, taking these as some sort of absolutes? Ought we not to be asking questions here too?

This is what is in fact happening among groups of modern theologians. Just to take over the tradition of the past is no longer enough.

I decided that alongside of teaching academic theology I would try to ask myself how far and in what way a doctrine of the creed or a saying of Christ had become part of what I am. The pulpit seemed the obvious place from which to expound what I thus discovered. And I resolved that I would not preach about any aspect of Christian belief unless it had become part of my own life-blood. For I realized that the Christian truth I tried to proclaim would speak to those who listened only to the degree in which it was an expression of my own identity. Previously, it seemed to me, I had often been like a man who, while perhaps he enjoyed a good tune, was essentially unmusical and who attempted from the books he had read to describe the quality of Beethoven's quartets. And I wondered how much I had thereby contributed to the emptying of the Churches by making the Christian gospel appear unreal and irrelevant to people's lives.[8]

To attempt to make Christianity come alive in this way may sometimes seem destructive, for the questions it may prompt will sometimes seem irreverent, if not blasphemous. To ask whether people in the past got things right may seem to make our age the criteria for all things and even to sit in judgment on our betters, perhaps forgetting the others who will come after to judge us. But to accept beliefs untested is just not compatible with our understanding of the demands of a twentieth-century search for truth.

Is a doctrine of the Incarnation really necessary for a true understanding of the nature of Christian belief? Can any convincing reason be given why God should be thought of as being in three persons, neither less nor more – given the rich manifoldness of the functions and activities attributed to him, why should the number of his persons not be increased indefinitely? Can any way be found of stating convincingly how the act of one person in the past can atone for all the sins of the world, actual and potential?

These are questions which are now being freely discussed, not in any light-hearted or negative way but in an attempt to see precisely what form of belief Christianity now entails.[9] Instead of resisting the process, as the church seems so often to be doing at present, would it not be better for it to give the new developments full rein and indeed encourage them, in the thought that even this might be from God? In belief, above all things, does the church not need to be far more relaxed, understanding and open?

The dogmatic hurdles at the entrance to the Church succeed in doing only two things: they let in people who for the most part have made a purely mental and superficial assent to the formularies, and who then spend their lives putting on an act, an external and artificial mimicking of a way of life that is spontaneous or nothing; and they keep out a great many people in whom the root of love is growing and flowering but who for one reason or another cannot commit themselves sincerely to the full dogmatic faith of the Church. In this way those inside are cut off from the very fellowship which would help them to mature in love (how many congregations there are, for example, which cannot carry out even the childishly simple project of a Christmas bazaar without enough envy, hatred, and malice to power a dozen major crimes), and those outside are denied the opportunity to move towards a real understanding of the faith. Everyone gets the worst of all possible worlds; and only an open church offers any hope of putting this right.[10]

5

Come to Church

'We are being called, over the years ahead, to far more than a restating of traditional orthodoxy in modern terms. Indeed, if our defence of the Faith is limited to this, we shall find in all likelihood that we have lost out to all but a tiny religious remnant. A much more radical recasting, I would judge, is demanded, in the process of which the most fundamental categories of our theology – of God, of the supernatural, and of religion itself – must go into the melting.'[1]

Though the significance of our understanding that history offers no firm resting points for faith, even in the Bible, Jesus or Christian doctrine, was not drawn out in *Honest to God*, taking that understanding seriously calls for a revolution which is quite as radical. As we have seen, it means looking once again at the legacies of the past with new eyes and asking 'What is the place of this, or that, in the life and belief of the church? How can we make it our own?' Detailed discussions of what that might involve will be found elsewhere, and all the intellectual consequences for our thinking cannot be pursued now.

One point, however, must be taken further. Suppose it is accepted that the best way of understanding the Bible, Jesus and Christian doctrine is in historical terms, along the lines drawn in the previous chapter (and if this is not the best way, then let us have a clearly-written account of the alternative, in language and ideas that can be clearly understood), then surely something must be done about the way in which Christians spend the time when they come together for worship. For where so much needs to be learnt and rethought, where we have for so long accepted so much second-hand from the past, there is an urgent need for new kinds of community activity, in learning and worship, far beyond anything which has so far been attempted.

Consider the average occasion on which the local church gathers for worship, once a week, on a Sunday. Within the hour or so during which it is together it will have passages from the Bible read as though they were speaking directly from the past to the present; it will join together in saying a creed which, although supposedly rephrased in modern terminology, comes from a very different past; like generations before it, it will be instructed by means of a sermon, though methods of teaching have changed out of all recognition since the time when public speaking was virtually the only means of instruction; it will share in the celebration of the eucharist, the central symbolic action of the Christian church down the ages and once prepared for with great care, but now often treated so casually that there is a yawning gap between the words and actions of the service which presuppose it taking place in the family of God, and the very real superficiality of personal contact among the congregation; and it will sing hymns the sentiments of which, pondered in cold blood, often go against anything which might be said to be the gospel; and in all this it will be expected to grow in mutual friendship and in Christian understanding.

Of course there ought to be more occasion for meeting than this. But usually there is not, and one prominent reason is the lack of any indication within the service that there is so much more to be explored and to be thought and said. In most worship there is little reflection of the searching, the questioning, the wondering, the puzzlement which make up so much of what we feel to be our authentic religious experience. Everything is certainty, assurance, affirmation.

The language of worship, of creed, of liturgy, still essentially in a traditional form, constantly sets out to claim too much. Its language is time and again the language of finality, its tone the tone of supreme authority. It has a tendency to present its doctrines and its exhortations from the standpoint of God, which is one that we cannot possibly take, even with what knowledge we have of the life and work of Jesus. And its complete oblivion to the sort of questions which were raised in the previous chapter means that at the one time when Christians do meet together in any numbers they are brainwashed into looking at God, their faith and the world in terms which just do not fit any coherent explanations that can be given.

Now it is very easy to make fun of what worship would be like if the more radical theologians had their way with it.

> Hark the herald angels sing:
> 'Bultmann is the latest thing!'
> (Or they would if he had not
> Demythologized the lot.)
> Joyful, all ye nations rise,
> Glad to existentialize!
> Peace on earth and mercy mild,
> God and Science reconciled.[2]

But fun of this kind is cheap fun, like the exaggerated cheering with which audiences greet someone who has laughed down a point that has troubled them.

Of course when we are engaged in worship we are involved in the language of poetry and myth, we are using evocative statements which hint at what cannot be said, and are using images and archetypes which affect us at levels far below that of our conscious mind. (And it is a pity that some of those concerned with revising public worship have not been more aware of this.) But we are also concerned with the truth, and there is a good deal in the pattern of our worship that is so much in tension with what seems as though it might be the truth that to anyone attempting to work out for him or herself a form of Christianity that makes sense, it cries out for change.

Strangely, this is not in fact an argument for a completely new start. It is possible to feel this way and still delight in the ceremonial of, say, Anglican cathedral evensong and the great liturgical services of the church's year. In the same way as concerts, or plays, or operas, these can still reach parts of our being which other features of our modern world pass by (and we are now moving back towards what was said at the end of chapter 2). Truth of a kind can be communicated to us in this way in a manner which we might be hard put to explain. We can emerge from such worship changed and refreshed and seeing the world in yet another perspective, as we can on a return from those other activities – from revisiting the ancient world to walking on the hills – that give us new vision. But everything needs to be put in a meaningful framework, needs to go to reinforce a pattern of belief which will be a recognizable, honest and authentic Christian faith for our times. And at this point too much of what goes on in the churches just does not stand the test.

To see where a cluster of unresolved problems still remains, related to those we looked at in the last chapter but now much more in the realm of the church's practice than the church's belief, for the rest of this chapter we shall just look around the church and its worship and organization, and ask some questions.

First, to conclude the discussion of the last chapter. In the light of what we have seen about the way in which Bible, doctrine and the words of Jesus belong to the past and with their time, do we not need to think much harder about which biblical readings, creeds, and statements about Jesus are used? Of course we will expect to go back time and again to the life and work of Jesus, to the history of the people of Israel which led up to him and the first Christians who followed him, but will we not do this better if we do it with a little more consideration? Ought we not, as members of a family which stretches back over the centuries, to make our family gatherings much more varied and wide-ranging affairs; never far from the focal events of Christianity but commemorating also the other great stages along the course which has brought us where we are? Ought we not, even in worship, to train ourselves more at moving backwards and forwards between our own time and a past which is a real past, seeing it in its own light and allowing it to stand as a measure against the life and thought of our own age? Whatever our answers to suggestions of this kind, what is our justification for keeping to so many old and by now stale patterns, when there are so many other possibilities that we have not even begun to try?

Words and thoughts go to make up the expression of Christian doctrine, but so too do actions, which can be expressed in more permanent form in types of ministry and sacramental ceremonies. Children are baptized with water in the name of the Father, the Son and the Holy Spirit; in some churches hands are laid on them by the bishop before they are admitted to full membership of the church; the eucharist is celebrated by the breaking of bread and blessing of wine; men are set apart for the ordained ministry by ordination.

None of these institutions, however, is now without its problems, and in addition they are just as much factors which make for division as some of the more abstract doctrines that we considered earlier.

For example, baptism is common to all Christian churches and its validity is generally recognized, but there is considerable discussion about just when it should be administered: many churches baptize children soon after they are born, with sponsors making promises on behalf of those baptized until they are able to answer for themselves, while other churches have protested that such a view is illegitimate and that only those should be baptized who are old enough to understand what it means. The argument has ranged to and fro over a long period with a good deal to be said on each side and with no obvious solution. The eucharist too is celebrated, under different names, throughout the churches, but again there are very different understandings of precisely what is taking place or how it is achieved or by whom the eucharist may be performed. Is the main emphasis to be on the people who gather together, with the element of the meal as a secondary feature, or is the emphasis on the consecrated priest and his action with the bread and wine which changes them into something that they were not before? With these different understandings go different views of the ministry, so that in some traditions there are bishops and a hierarchy, with stress on continuity of ordination, whereas in, say, the churches which grew up after the Reformation, the function of the minister is viewed in very different terms.

These are the counters which are juggled around in attempts to reach agreements between the churches in ecumenical discussions and in attempts at revised forms of worship. The desire for closer relationship between the churches inevitably raises the question of the nature of the ministry, while the call for a revision of baptismal and confirmation services, as well as the eucharist, calls for some understanding of precisely what it is that is being presented in a new form.

Yet here, as we saw earlier, is one of the strangest gaps of all. For all the urgency of these essentially practical questions, there is virtually no indication, at least in books and public statements, that there is a real understanding within the churches, which can be communicated in modern ideas and terminology, of what baptism, confirmation, the eucharist are, and why they should have one form or be administered in one way and not another. As with the more abstract questions of doctrine, it is possible to find books which recount the history of these practices, which indicate how they became what they have become, but there is nothing which indicates what they actually are.

Take baptism as an example. In 1965 the Parish and People Movement sponsored an ecumenical conference entitled 'Crisis for Baptism', the papers of which were later published. Contributors came from the Baptist, Congregationalist, Serbian Orthodox and Roman Catholic churches, the Church of England, the Church of Scotland, and the Society of Friends. Papers considered virtually every aspect of the practice of baptism, and there was a report of discussions and comment. Yet summing up, the last speaker found himself having to be very negative in his judgments.

I have been somewhat surprised by the way people sometimes seem to have taken it for granted that we do all know what actually happens in baptism. Questions like, 'What is given in confirmation which is not already given in baptism?' have been asked, and the question has seemed to presume that we know what is already given in baptism. Indeed, there was, I thought, a surprising degree of agreement yesterday with Fr Davis when he said: 'There is one Spirit and one indwelling of the Spirit which is given at baptism.' Now I know that this is biblical language, and I know that it is the biblical language which has been used in the church for centuries. But as a child of our time I do not really understand it; and, to be honest, if it means what it seems to mean, I simply do not believe it. And I find myself wondering how many of you really believe that a baptised person – infant, child or adult – is 'indwelt by the Spirit' after they have been baptised, but that (by implication) an unbaptised person is not. In fact I have been greatly surprised that in this Conference so little attention has been given to this question of mythology, to demythologizing and remythologizing. For frankly, until I know rather more precisely what happens in baptism, and until I am persuaded rather more certainly that we together know what happens, I doubt whether I can get all that worked up about tidying up baptismal policy. Certainly, while we are content to speak of this 'indwelling of the Spirit' in the way we have spoken of it, it will all to my mind remain a kind of discussion for an 'in-group', far removed from the way people in the world at large think and speak of humanity.[3]

If there has been a convincing answer to these questions raised by Eric James more than ten years ago, I do not know where to find it. And do the questions still trouble the churches? If so, how are they to be resolved? At least at that time they were being asked, whereas now silence seems to have fallen again.

During the same period there was also vigorous discussion about the future of confirmation, and this too was published in book form. Theologians, educationalists, parish clergy, sociologists, psychologists, industrial chaplains all made their contributions, but the result was hardly more encouraging. 'It is clear,' wrote the editor, 'that whereas a few years ago the Church thought it knew exactly what it was doing in preparing young people for Confirmation, in confirming them, and in catering for their needs, nowadays we are ready to admit to an almost complete bewilderment on this score. Yet the reason does not lie in neglect of their duty on the part of the clergy. It is probably true to say that parish priests and chaplains have never taken Confirmation preparation and after-care so seriously as in the present generation.'[4]

The problem does not need to be elaborated. But confirmation does illustrate one factor which we have not yet come across in looking at the way in which the churches acquired their present doctrines and practices, a factor which is of considerable importance.

By now, if we ask 'what is confirmation?', we will expect only a historical answer in terms of how it came to be. But here, as elsewhere, we shall find that this historical development was governed not only by the working out of a theological principle; sheer practical necessity played its part, and the theology was bent to fit.

The entry on 'Confirmation' in the *Oxford Dictionary of the Christian Church* itself illustrates the confusion that there is here. How confirmation began is easy enough to see. Originally membership of the church was by baptism and a profession of faith, but as time went on and infants were baptized into the church, the need arose for a separate ceremony to mark the point at which an individual himself or herself made a responsible decision to become a member of the church and to make a profession of faith. But then some theological explanation had to be thought up for what happened in this second ceremony, and for the way in which it was related to the first, and from this point on there is considerable difference of opinion and argument in the various traditions.

Applied theology, that is, the theology behind the various customs, practices and institutions of the church, is in fact a jungle of bad arguments, precisely because it is often a case of finding a theological explanation of something which has arisen for quite other reasons. Religion comes before theology, and practice tends to come before theory. Sacrifice, for example, was offered for millennia before anyone asked how it could be thought efficacious, and no satisfactory answer has yet been given. And the history of Christian rites and institutions often makes us very much aware of the gulf between historical explanations of how they have arrived at their present form and the theological reasons that have been given in the past for it.[5]

This is very much the case with the ordained ministry. Why should there be an ordained ministry at all? The preface to 'The Form and Manner of Making, Ordaining, and Consecrating of Bishops, Priests, and Deacons according to the order of the Church of England' states with confidence that 'it is evident unto all men diligently reading holy Scripture and ancient Authors that from the Apostles' times there have been these Orders of Ministers in Christ's Church; Bishops, Priests and Deacons'. Yet this is very far from being the case. More recent studies have made it quite clear that this threefold ministry was in fact a secondary development out of a much more diverse and variegated church order; it became dominant in the church during the second century, and did so above all for non-theological reasons. In particular, there was a desire for order and a need to cope with the growing number of Christians.

A brief illustration highlights as well as anything could the way in which these practical questions could become dominant:

> If you invite a small number of relations or friends to your house, you will ask them to sit down at your table and you yourself will serve them ... If fifty people come you would alter the time of the occasion and would arrange for refreshments ... If two hundred people are invited you would put the matter into the hands of professional caterers and you would greet personally only some of your guests and make a little speech.[6]

Many things happened within the churches simply because they grew larger and because their place in society changed. And so, among other things, the clerical profession arose and with it the professional consciousness which goes with all professional people, and the sense of status, so that the clergy began to think of their position in terms of personal power – power to celebrate the sacraments and power to regulate the life of the church.

A verse in Mrs Alexander's well-known hymn 'All things bright and beautiful' which is often left out of hymnals nowadays reflects another consequence of this development.

The rich man in his castle, the poor man at the gate,
God made them high and lowly, and ordered their estate.

Something of this kind of thinking became associated with the ideology of the ministry. Men were permanently set aside according to their class and function, and this was divinely ordained. Once a man had been given his position or had been called to it, there he was and there he stayed. And so there was a rigidly defined line between clergy and laity.

But what becomes of the doctrine of the ministry when the overall pattern of society has changed out of all recognition and the old pattern of divinely ordered positions has been abandoned? What happens to a doctrine of the ministry when society is no longer static, but mobile and subject to rapid change? The results are there to be seen. In today's society the ordained minister is more often than not an odd man out, involved in great personal tension over what he should or should not do, puzzled over his status and above all isolated and removed from the general life of society, following a completely different life-style and being robbed by virtue of his status of the involvement with other people which he so much needs.[7]

If practical considerations played their part in the rise of a theology of the ordained ministry, in a healthy church now would surely be the time when they should come to the fore again, when there should be far more thinking about precisely what the nature of priesthood is. For if one thing is certain, it is that within our complex society there can be no effective leadership from those who by their very calling are cut off from direct involvement in its complexities and are banished to a somewhat insecure place right on the periphery.

As we have seen, it is very difficult indeed for clergy themselves to ask questions. After all, it is their way of life, their career, their raison d'être which is at stake. It may well be that really deep thought on the nature of the ministry as it should now be understood will bring considerable suffering and disillusionment to those who have looked upon it in a conventional way. But there is suffering and disillusionment already, and it is no service to future generations if an unsatisfactory situation is allowed to drag on when change and new thinking are what is really needed. The nature of ordination and the status of the ordained ministry cannot just be left as a time-honoured mystique: it needs to be investigated much more thoroughly.

But, it will be argued, one thing at least is clear. The minister is ordained to be minister of the word and the sacrament. Does not a special place remain for him here?

What the ministry of the word involves in modern society is, as we have seen, a complex matter; but nothing that we have come across so far necessarily leads us to suppose that the ordained minister has a special gift in preaching or teaching that cannot be found in others. Indeed, part of the present crisis is that others may well be better qualified at these things than he. The best sermon I have ever heard was preached by a layman; teachers in schools, colleges and universities may have a far more thorough grounding in theology than parish clergy, nor is deep knowledge of the spiritual life confined to those who are ordained.

And questions are beginning to arise over the role of the ordained minister at the eucharist. It may be expedient in terms of church discipline that every eucharist should be presided over by an ordained minister. But it is now clear that we do not know enough about the nature of the eucharist to say that this is theologically necessary. For another of those questions which it seems that we are no longer capable of answering is 'What is it that the eucharist in fact is?'

For centuries the eucharist, the sharing of bread and wine after the example of Jesus at the last supper, has been the focal point of violent controversy and dissension. It is still impossible for those who have grown up in different Christian traditions to meet together in this way without being disobedient to the official regulations of their churches. Yet if one thing is clear, it is that in our present state of knowledge we cannot be so dogmatic as to lay down detailed rules about what does or does not make up a valid eucharist. And what is the meaning of 'validity' anyway? Is it possible to control the working of God's grace as it is believed to come through the eucharist in these terms?

68

As in other areas of church life, in the eucharist we inherit from the past a rich variety of practice and understanding which cannot be expressed in any single form. The eucharist is celebrated formally, and with great ceremony, in crowded cathedrals on the major festivals; it is celebrated quietly, almost impersonally, in churches early on Sunday mornings, week by week; it is celebrated informally, among groups of people who work or live together, as the best expression they can give, in an age which is poor in ways of expressing its deepest feelings, in offices or in private houses. Perhaps we are unable to say much at all about what it means, but we must try somehow to understand what it is that we are asserting in this variety; and what will surely emerge, here as elsewhere, is that we may be freer than we think, even here, and that God's action too is freer and less tied to particular forms or specific details. Understanding of the eucharist, it has been suggested,

> may be illustrated by an analogy with the multiplicity of meanings to be found in Beethoven's string quartets. Their central importance for music is generally agreed. Yet it is hard to formulate what they mean in words, precisely because they are already formulated in music. So the eucharist should be expected to have a wide range of interpretation. This does not mean that there cannot be false interpretations. The wide range of admissible interpretations of the string quartets does not mean that there are not ways of taking them which are quite wrong. So there are ways of interpreting the eucharist which must be excluded as wrong – ways, for example, which omit the transcendent dimension or the redemptive element altogether. But it does mean that no one interpretation can be claimed as the true interpretation, thereby excluding all others which cannot be fully harmonized with it.[8]

Going on from this conviction, Maurice Wiles, who makes the comparison, can argue that in our present circumstances a wide variety of eucharistic practice is possible, allowing in particular circumstances both for eucharists without an ordained minister as celebrant and for intercommunion.

What should happen to the eucharist, he points out, would run parallel to changes in our understanding of the nature of the church. While it used to seem self-evident that in the face of the divided churches it was appropriate to ask which was a church and which was not, experience of the way in which God's grace could be seen operating in Christian bodies outside the 'true church' has led to a completely different perspective on the question. Now many would prefer to speak in terms of the degree to which differing Christian bodies do or do not express in their life and structure the marks to be looked for in the church as a norm. In a similar way, we need perhaps be less concerned even over drawing boundaries of what is or what is not a genuine eucharist and learn from the different ways in which we can come together.

If the eucharist does present a problem on many occasions, it is because of the nature of the church which it presupposes. Here, the eucharist seems to say, is the family of God meeting together to strengthen its mutual love and reconciliation. Furthermore, there is a fashion now for theologies which talk of the whole church as being the people of God, and of the priesthood of all believers; but like the eucharist, they often seem to remain no more than fine words within the structures of the church as they now are. And here again we come close to some of the points made in earlier chapters.

John Macquarrie wrote a popular, much-read book entitled *The Faith of the People of God*. In it, he argued that all theology ought to be 'lay' theology in the widest sense of the word, that is, developed from the experience of the people of God, by the people of God, for the people of God. But how can one talk of 'the people of God', of 'the church' as a basis for theology, indeed as an identifiable group of people who actually exist and can be involved in this kind of theology, when the reality is more likely to be close to the picture presented at the beginning of this chapter?

Doubtless there are churches which hold together as communities, which can honestly claim to share common beliefs and common styles of life, but experience shows that they may well be unrepresentative. Many churches find great difficulty in being a community of any kind; members may attend at irregular intervals, and even the most regular are quite likely to differ strongly among themselves in beliefs, practices and priorities. This is something that we have already noticed.

The church as it is, is rather the organization that we met in the first and third chapters, desperately in need of those groups which can hardly be said to be of the church, and in particular of those with virtually no formal connection with the churches, who are nevertheless interested in religious questions and whose lives often show impressive signs of commitment.

Community, the sense of family, the sense of welcoming openness, is something which – as we have seen – the churches are not prepared to give enough attention to and take enough trouble over. Part of the reason may well be that those who talk about the church are so influenced by the high-flown language applied to it from the past that they fail to see the gulf between the ideal and the reality. There is a constant tendency in church tradition to define the church in terms other than it really is – holy, the body of Christ, his heavenly bride, the new human race, the family for which Jesus was betrayed – and to expect that somehow theology and the grace of God will bridge the gap between this and what the church actually is. St Paul might seem to encourage this with his idealistic language about the all-too-human communities of the churches which he helped to found, but this can surely never be an excuse for today.[9] There is no other church than the church which we see around us, and there is no way of becoming that church apart from our own involvement, sharing, caring in human terms. Perhaps the real problem that we have been facing in this chapter is the place of symbolism in a community where the reality which should match that symbol has almost died away. Perhaps what is needed to make sense of worship, ministry, sacraments and church is a change in the community, an altera-tion in its way of life far beyond anything that has hitherto been accomplished. And it is no good leaving such a change to what God might be expected to do, simply waiting and hoping for some new descent of the Holy Spirit.

6

Voices in the Wilderness

Running through this book right from the beginning have been two parallel but related sets of questions. Has the church now become the kind of organization whose make-up in fact gets in the way of its calling to create caring communities and display an outward-looking love, and are the beliefs which it professes by now little more than a formality, with no real life in them? In either case, is what we have left a shell, rather than an organism capable of changing and developing in a new way?

Pursuing these two themes may seem to have involved us in a great deal of demolition work, and by this point the thoughtful reader may have begun to feel that the only possible ending must be one of unutterable gloom. After all that has been said, if there is any truth at all in it, what can possibly be left of Christian belief? This chapter will attempt to pick up some pieces.

Right at the start, we should remind ourselves once again what it is that we are concerned about. Religious belief is a matter of life and death, part of a search for ultimate reality which involves the mind, the emotions and the heart, a search which means looking for the truth about ourselves, who we are, and what the reason is for our being here at all. Such a search and such a concern demands all that we can possibly give. It cannot be content with anything once it has been shown to be either unintelligible phraseology or less than the truth. God – if he is – is better than that. And if much of the apparent intellectual substance of Christianity as it is now presented falls into either of these two inadequate categories, then we have to think and look and search and respond again, however difficult and however unpalatable that may be. For us, the famous words in St John's Gospel, 'the spirit will lead you into all truth and the truth will make you free', cannot add up to the conclusion that Christianity in something like its traditional form is inevitably true no matter what. It must mean, rather, that we should be willing, in hope, to follow the quest for truth wherever it seems to lead.

Similarly, if the organized communities which call themselves Christian churches do in fact prove so little capable of drawing from us the best that we can give of ourselves in time and energy and effective care and loving concern, and so little able to give of friendship and acceptance and encouragement and inspiration where these are so badly needed, then we must be ruthless in asking why, and not stop at the asking, but attempt to do something in practice.

Perhaps this is the best point at which to say something about the general outlines of the picture presented in this book, about the questions that have been asked and the evidence and authority for some of the assumptions that have been made. Nothing here is particularly new. The thoughts, the illustrations and the comments are certainly not original. Scarcely a statement here could not be found in the writings of others, many of them holding prominent positions in academic theology or as leaders of the church. The footnotes record the most obvious borrowings; for the rest, I gladly acknowledge that most of the time I have absorbed comments, tested them against my own experience, tried to recall them here, collect them together and present them within a limited compass.

The attempt might have been made at much greater length and in much greater detail but that would almost certainly have resulted in yet another long and rather technical book. The brevity of much of the discussion and the way in which it has moved from one topic to another may have made some of the writing seem little more than impressionistic and verging on the incoherent; but if it succeeds in opening up more conversations over at least some of the issues, it will have served its purpose.

These further conversations are urgently needed. For while the questions that have been raised here have been current in the churches, some for well over a decade, and others for an even longer period in the past, they do not seem to have penetrated very far. They are usually taken, to judge from public attitudes, as minority opinions, as isolated divergences from what is still thought to be a viable structure of belief and practice. They are, if you like, 'voices in the wilderness', the thoughts of the odd men out. And there are many who wish that a way could be found to stop them troubling the faith of the 'simple believers' and to leave the churches in peace.

Against this, what I have tried to suggest is that the cumulative effect of all this questioning when it is seen in concentrated form, the number of problems which appear at almost every turn, and the general ineffectiveness and deadness of the churches mean that the whole balance of presuppositions has now shifted. Those who think that traditional Christian belief and the traditional way of life within the churches can be taken for granted and that individual questions can be parried and warded off one by one need more to defend their opinions than reliance on past habit, inertia and the status quo. In the present situation they need to provide a more comprehensible justification for what they continue to uphold and to assume. And they need to ask themselves just how representative a figure the 'simple believer' is; on closer acquaintance many people will prove to be made in a very different mould.

The argument, then, could be more detailed and thorough, and its content is not particularly original. But just as the points I have tried to make and the questions I have tried to raise are often prompted, in the form in which I have raised them, from elsewhere, so too there are other places where they can be verified and pursued at greater length. I would be quite happy for everything that has been said here, every problem that has been posed, to have a question mark put against it. But once the question has been formed, then let the answer be given, clearly and relevantly. That can do nothing but good all round. And let the answer be not only in intellectual terms, but in practical ones too.

A good deal may have been questioned, but there is also a good deal that has not. The questions which have been asked here have been directed against many of the forms in which Christianity is now expressed rather than against its innermost content and the most profound levels of Christian experience. There has been no questioning of the realities of what can still be seen as a recognizably Christian life lived today: the strength that is given people from beyond their own resources to achieve what they might not have been able to achieve unaided, what we might call the work of the Holy Spirit. There has been no questioning of the realities of love and forgiveness and reconciliation. There has been no suggestion that the Christian tradition as a whole may not have a wealth of material which we need to attempt to understand, that there are those within it, from the past and the present, who know a great deal better than we do and from whom we need to learn. There has been no questioning of the ultimate importance of prayer and worship and the dimensions they might possibly open up for us. There has been no questioning of the place within Christianity of the Bible and of Jesus – provided that in each case we are careful to think about what we have and about the certainties that we have *not* been given. Finally, there has been no questioning of the meaningfulness of talking about God or of belief in him, though in the freedom that we have been given and by the very nature of that belief we may often be plunged into abysses of doubt and despair.

In fact, I feel sure that in this dimension we are more fortunate than many generations who have gone before us. In both intellectual terms and in terms of the way in which we live and react towards one another, our beliefs have been subjected to more testing over the most recent period than ever before in the history of Christianity. And they have withstood the test. Often we may not be sure how to put what we feel into words; as I said at the end of the first chapter, we may be lacking the right forms with which to express the workings of the Spirit, the right language in which to express those things which touch us most deeply. Nevertheless, for those who have the eyes to see, the insight, the understanding, the realities of daily living which Christians have described in different terms down the ages are still very much there, and can come upon us when we least expect it.

That does not, of course, mean that at this late stage in the discussion it is possible to set everything to rights by a new twist in the argument, removing at a stroke the difficulties that have arisen. But it does put them in a new perspective. And that makes all the difference. It is when we are uncertain, puzzled, unhappy that we have to cling on to the old forms and the old structures because they are all that we have and we need our belief bolstered up by props of this kind. When the dimensions of faith, hope, love, forgiveness become real to us, we are given at the same time a freedom, an openness towards a way of living which is quite new. And we can see many of the familiar features of Christian thinking and practice for what they are: the attempts of previous generations to put into effect what they have seen of God through Jesus and that long series of events, ideas, individuals and communities for whom he has been a focal point, *in their own terms.* We may admire and respect these attempts for what they are. We may seek to understand them to the best of our ability. We may enter into the spirit of them and find our imaginations stimulated and our horizons broadened; we may see them as all too human mistakes and vow not to fall into the same trap again. But at the same time we shall find ourselves standing at one remove from them, simply because the attempts are not, and cannot be ours. They belong to the past, and for life in the present we look for a pattern of faith and life which is ours and not borrowed at second hand from someone else.

What we have to look for is the right way for us, in our time, to express as far as possible what we believe other generations to have struggled to express in different and even alien terms, making many mistakes in the process. Indeed, this is the only way in which we shall be able to share it effectively with our own contemporaries. If ours is a faith which is constantly in search of understanding, then we need to look once again for words and ideas and ways of living and caring which make sense to us and enable us to pass on that good news which is supposed to be our prize possession.

76

Those aspects of Christianity which have not been questioned here might be said to be its essential characteristics; they may take different forms and be expressed among different groups in each period of history, but they really do seem to have withstood the test of experience over the centuries and to keep emerging, if not as certainties (which we have not been given), at least as points in the bedrock of our existence where our questions, rather than seeming to destroy and demolish, almost unexpectedly turn back on us and take, in the end, a positive form. For here, in the last resort, we find that we are no longer in control of the questioning but are ourselves put to the test. Who are you? Why are you here? Where are you going? Why is your world as it is? What is real for you? Why is it that you are drawn towards that ultimate reality whom men call God?

As we have seen, in the past confident answers of one kind or another have been given to all these questions. Christianity indeed has sought to provide a full explanation of man's nature and destiny, his salvation and his future state, and has given instructions about what is necessary for his eternal well-being. But the form in which these answers have been given has come increasingly to seem at best second-hand or obscure, at worst restrictive and over-dogmatic.

Now he would be a rash person who scorned all past experience, but there have been many pointers in this book suggesting that for our time the best expression of faith may in fact be the asking of questions and following where they lead, rather than the blind acceptance of what has come down to us from elsewhere. This may be our best hope of finding a way to shape new patterns of living and believing. After all, there are many indications that in almost every respect ours is an age that is all too ready to be fobbed off with half-truth, and if ultimate questions about life and death and values and purpose do have the quality that I have suggested, then to press on towards them, even if we do not see what the outcome could be, might be a way of provoking change not only within Christianity, but outside it as well. There are plenty of questions that Christians can ask others about the way in which they live, about their attitude to the world and to each other, about the use of natural resources – but only if they have first gone through the experience of a radical questioning of themselves.

There is a point at which our ultimate questions turn round and question us. Ironically, it is a sociologist rather than a theologian who has brought this home in the most vivid way:

> A child wakes up in the night, perhaps from a bad dream, and finds himself surrounded by darkness, alone, beset by nameless threats. At such a moment the contours of trusted reality are blurred or invisible, and in the terror of incipient chaos the child cries out for his mother. It is hardly an exaggeration to say that at this moment, the mother is being invoked as a high priestess of protective order. It is she (and, in many cases, she alone) who has the power to banish the chaos and to restore the benign shape of the world. And, of course, any good mother will do just that. She will take the child and cradle him in the timeless gesture of the Magna Mater who became our Madonna. She will turn on a lamp, perhaps, which will encircle the scene with a warm glow of reassuring light. She will speak or sing to the child, and the content of this communication will invariably be the same – 'Don't be afraid – everything is in order, everything is all right.' If all goes well, the child will be reassured, his trust in reality recovered, and in this trust he will return to sleep.[1]

A common enough scene, yet it raises one of those questions which we have seen as fundamental to our very existence. Is what the mother says true, or is she lying to the child? The mother's actions are true only if there is some truth to the religious understanding of human existence. For if reality is limited to the natural reality that we see around us, then the reassurance given to the child, as it may be given to other people in other situations, even on a deathbed or by a graveside, is ultimately a lie. For all is not well. The terror which the child is experiencing is the ultimate reality, and the reassurance given is no more than a diversion. At the heart of the process which is essential to the making of a human person, at one of the most crucial moments of trust, there is a lie.

78

A transposition of this argument into more formally religious terms is easy enough. Down the centuries, Christians have worshipped God, prayed to him, believed in his ultimate providence. The life of Jesus makes no sense at all without God, dominated as it is by this pattern. Is all this a response to a God who is? Or is it an illusion? There is no third possibility. If God is an illusion, then the prayer, worship, belief of past centuries and of our own time are illusions too, and we need to change our ways, for it is foolish to follow illusions. But if God is not an illusion, then in the end of the day everything is not left to us, but is finally taken out of our hands.

And if God is, then we are freed from the dreadful concern that if our religion is not just right, if we have not followed prescriptions or ritual or inherited patterns down to the last detail, then in some way we have lost him. Christianity, with its emphasis on love and freedom, with the love of the outcast shown by Jesus, has always had within it the seeds of extravagant recklessness, of apparent irresponsibility towards the demands of law and morality. And as a result there have always been those who have attempted to safeguard it with the protection of rules and regulations, hierarchies and rituals. But is not a feature of this development which we are now seeing all too clearly a kind of introverted legalism, a fearfulness, a lack of joy, a lack of freedom, an assertiveness which in the last analysis is essentially selfish and man-centred?

So much of religious literature and religious questioning and religious practice in the end focuses on anxieties like 'will *I* be saved?', 'can *I* be sure?', 'what is *my* future?' Which only stresses the point. By contrast, it is interesting that the illustration of the mother reassuring the child given by Peter Berger is wholly in terms of one person reassuring someone else. And when we recognize this we may find the imaginary scene strikes home in more than one respect. For the real question, the question we find ourselves asking when we truly love, truly care, is not a self-centred one: 'what will happen to *me*'? That becomes of relatively minor and secondary importance. What really matters is: what will happen to *him*? What will happen to *her*?

79

Questioning, then, can prove to be more than just a restless and uncommitted agnosticism; it can take us to the heart of things and at least leave us struggling for the rest of our lives with those pointers which somehow refuse to allow us to say with finality 'There is no God.' And it need not reflect chronic anxiety about one's own ultimate fate: it can be a real expression of care and love and concern for others. And because we are given at least some indication that in the last resort we shall not find that everything is entirely up to us, the result of questioning can be liberation, openness, even laughter, because when the last question has been asked it is just not true that there is nothing there.

Laughter is not a sound that is often heard in the churches, and when it does occur it is often forced. And yet, when one reflects, true laughter is *the* sure sign that all is well. Many of us will be fortunate enough to know of places where it is more common. Here, at any rate, is one testimony:

> There are homes one enjoys visiting and regrets leaving. The gaiety and sincerity, the sanity and reliability, of the people who live in them, their readiness to attend or to help, and to think the best of others, mean that they are always the one turned to in a crisis, and that their lives are constantly loaded with new burdens never shown by them to be so. There are other groups where in their own special circumstances recognizably the same air is abroad: shops, offices, small businesses, common rooms, schools, committees. Membership of any such group can induce in an individual the change which he needs but cannot impose upon himself. It can change him so radically that long after he has moved on, and has lost all contact with anyone in whom this spirit is present, he still feels it challenging by contrast the dark, formal, insensitive new wisdom of his new environment. 'We never had this trouble at X – we didn't do things this way.' [2]

There, if anywhere, is a blueprint for the churches – yet we shall be lucky if we find incredible John Baker's subsequent comment that within the churches this atmosphere and its liberating effects are to be found only rarely. We are all too likely to have had the experience that so often the churches, far from helping people to realize their potentialities as human beings, in fact dehumanize them and somehow make them less than they are.

But this brings us full circle, back to the scenes of the first chapter, the failures of the churches, their lingering death, the opening scene in Highgate cemetery and the words of Karl Marx: 'The philosophers have only interpreted the world in various ways; the point, however, is to change it.'

How? And into what?

The fact that these two questions have been left so vague need not deter us. After all, setting out somewhere without being very sure where you are going is not exactly a new idea in the history of Christianity – or Judaism for that matter. The important thing is not to be so tied down that you are incapable even of beginning to make the effort.

Perhaps the needed change which has been the theme of this book will happen, perhaps it will not. If it does, then we shall discover that new forms of church life will produce new insights and new forms of living which will by-pass many of the problems raised here, as other problems have been by-passed in earlier days because they have been made irrelevant. If it does not, then one final question will have to be asked, because it follows relentlessly from the whole argument of this book.

If the church really does seem to persist regardless in being so blind and so unyielding and so unloving by virtue of the rigidity of its structures and the consequences of its often thoughtless doctrines, must there not inevitably come a point when the arguments for continuing to remain a formal member of it lose their force? In that case, surely the only honest and consistent course is to leave it, and out of solidarity with those others for whom it will not care, go permanently into the wilderness and see whether, against the odds, the age-old hopes of the prophets might again find their beginnings there.

Notes

Chapter 1

1. Alison Stuart, 'The Loneliness of Doubt', first published in *New Christian* in 1966 and reprinted in *A New Christian Reader*, edited by Lord Beaumont of Whitley, SCM Press 1974, pp. 59f.
2. John Hick, *Christianity at the Centre*, SCM Press 1968, pp. 77f.

Chapter 2

1. *The Honest to God Debate*, edited by John A. T. Robinson and David L. Edwards, SCM Press 1963, records contemporary reactions to *Honest to God* in some detail, quoting many of the first reviews.
2. Quoted in *The Honest to God Debate*, p. 40.
3. See John A. T. Robinson, *Honest to God*, SCM Press 1963, pp. 7, 10.
4. Philip Toynbee, *Towards the Holy Spirit*, SCM Press 1973, p. 79.
5. Peter Brook, *The Empty Space*, McGibbon & Kee 1968; Penguin Books 1972, p. 67.
6. Bernard Levin, *The Pendulum Years*, Cape 1970, p. 9.
7. Ibid., pp. 108f.
8. Ibid., pp. 369ff.

Chapter 3

1. Monica Furlong, *With Love to the Church*, Hodder 1965, p. 22.
2. John A. T. Robinson, *The New Reformation?*, SCM Press 1965, p. 16.
3. John A. T. Robinson, 'Look Back in Hope?', *Mowbrays Journal*, Spring 1977, pp. 3–8.

4. David E. Jenkins, *Living with Questions*, SCM Press 1969, p. 162.

5. Trevor Beeson, *The Church of England in Crisis*, Davis-Poynter 1973, pp. 123f.; the whole of chapter 7 is well worth reading on this point.

6. 'An Agreed Statement on Eucharistic Doctrine of the Anglican–Roman Catholic International Commission', quoted in *The Common Catechism*, Search Press 1975, p. 669.

7. T. G. A. Baker, *Questioning Worship*, SCM Press 1977, p. 8.

8. See James D. Smart, *The Strange Silence of the Bible in the Church*, SCM Press 1970, especially pp. 15ff.

Chapter 4

1. John Austin Baker, *The Foolishness of God*, Darton, Longman & Todd 1970, pp. 335f.; Fontana 1975, p. 343.

2. Albert Schweitzer, *The Quest of the Historical Jesus*, third edition, A. & C. Black 1954, p. 4.

3. John A. T. Robinson, *Honest to God*, p. 76.

4. John H. Hayes, *Son of God to Superstar: Twentieth-century Interpretations of Jesus*, Abingdon Press, Nashville 1976.

5. *Who was Jesus?*, a television programme master-minded by Don Cupitt, and first shown on BBC 2 in April 1977, is an excellent demonstration of this, standing in marked contrast to the Zeffirelli film shown earlier in the same month.

6. Carl Becker, *The Heavenly City of the Eighteenth Century Philosophers*, Yale University Press 1932, p. 19. The over-scrupulous should note that I have changed one name in this quotation, substituting St Paul for an original Dante to sharpen the point. The sense is not affected.

7. For greater discussion of many of the points touched on here see Dennis Nineham, *The Use and Abuse of the Bible*, Macmillan 1976; also John S. Dunne, *The Way of All the Earth*, Sheldon Press 1973, to which he refers in a most illuminating way.

8. H. A. Williams, *The True Wilderness*, Constable 1965, p. 8; for a triumphant vindication of the continued pursuit of this course see his *Tensions*, Mitchell Beazley 1976.

9. See especially Maurice Wiles, *The Remaking of Christian Doctrine*, SCM Press 1974, and *Working Papers in Doctrine*, SCM Press 1976, and *The Myth of God Incarnate*, edited by John Hick, SCM Press 1977.

10. John Austin Baker, *The Foolishness of God*, p. 328; Fontana edition p. 335.

Chapter 5

1. John A. T. Robinson, *Honest to God*, p. 7.

2. E. L. Mascall, 'Christmas with the Demythologizers', in *Pi in the High*, Faith Press 1959, p. 49.

3. Eric James, 'Reflections on the Conference', in *Crisis for Baptism*, edited by Basil S. Moss, SCM Press 1965, p. 129.

4. Michael Perry (ed), in *Crisis for Confirmation*, SCM Press 1967, p. 7.

5. See Don Cupitt, 'Theology and Practice', in *Crisis for Confirmation*, p. 98.

6. J. P. Audet, *Mariage et Celibat dans le service pastoral de l'Eglise*, Paris 1967, quoted in Victor de Waal, *What is the Church?*, SCM Press 1969, p. 104.

7. In connection with this discussion see especially Victor de Waal, *What is the Church?*, pp. 96–107.

8. Maurice Wiles, 'Eucharistic Theology – The Value of Diversity', in *Thinking about the Eucharist*, Essays by members of the Archbishops' Commission on Christian Doctrine, SCM Press 1972, p. 120. The whole essay raises a fascinating set of questions.

9. See John Austin Baker, 'The Myth of the Church', in *What about the New Testament?*, edited by Morna Hooker and Colin Hickling, SCM Press 1975, pp. 165–77.

Chapter 6

1. Peter L. Berger, *A Rumour of Angels*, Allen Lane: The Penguin Press 1970, p. 72.

2. John Austin Baker, *The Foolishness of God*, p. 319; Fontana edition p. 327.